American Jews
AND THE
Zionist Idea

American Jews
AND THE
Zionist Idea

Naomi W. Cohen

KTAV PUBLISHING HOUSE, INC.
1975

Library of Congress Cataloging in Publication Data

Cohen, Naomi Wiener, 1927-
  American Jews and the Zionist idea.

  Includes bibliographical references.
  1. Zionism—United States. 2. Jews in the United States—
Politics and government. 3. Israel and the Diaspora. I. Title.
DS149.C635   956.94'001   74-34267
ISBN 0-87068-272-5

MANUFACTURED IN THE UNITED STATES OF AMERICA

For
Gerson, Jeremy and Judy

CONTENTS

Preface

This study interprets the historical significance of Zionism within the American Jewish community from 1897 to 1967. Focusing on American Zionism as an integral part of the American matrix, the book emphasizes what Zionism has meant to American Jews, how it interacted with government policy and American social moods, and, above all, how Zionism was Americanized.

As such, it does not purport to be a history of the American Zionist movement. In the interests of brevity and overall interpretation it ignores many important figures who contributed to the development of Zionist thought and activity, and it pays little attention to the different ideologies and internal evolution of the numerous organizations which have made up the American Zionist movement. That story still awaits scholarly treatment.

I am grateful to Mrs. Sylvia Landress, director of the Zionist Archives and Library, and to Mr. Harry J. Alderman, director of the Blaustein Library, American Jewish Committee, for their numerous courtesies extended to me in the course of my research. Dr. Oscar Janowsky and Rabbi Abraham Karp read the completed manuscript and gave me the benefit of their insights and suggestions. The responsibility for any errors remains solely my own.

Hunter College of the City University
   of New York

NAOMI W. COHEN

Prologue

Political Zionism, the movement to establish a Jewish state in Palestine, was the culmination of the Jewish nationalist aspirations of the nineteenth century. It derived from sources both ancient and modern, but the result was a totally new entity. Its roots went back to age-old Jewish messianic thought, in which the return to the Holy Land was central, but Zionist ideology was secularist and marked a revolutionary break from the religious interpretation of Jewish existence. Zionism was also shaped by modern European nationalist thought, which spurred Jews on to dream of a national life like that of all the nations. But their movement differed from normal nationalism. One historian has properly called it "a maverick in the history of modern nationalism," [1] for it lacked a common land and language, which were the usual components of nationality and nationhood. Zionist aspirations reflected universalist teachings too, for the projected state rested on the values of human freedom and dignity. Since they despaired of Jews being able to enjoy the basic rights of man in society at large, Zionists sought to realize these goals through Jewish particularist means.

It was Theodor Herzl, an upper-middle-class, assimilated Western Jew who launched political Zionism. Herzl was born in Hungary in 1860. As a student of law at the University of Vienna, and later as a talented journalist and less talented playwright, he witnessed the upsurge of political and racial anti-Semitism in Austria, Germany, and France. The trial and public degradation of Captain Alfred Dreyfus (1894–95) for allegedly transmitting French military secrets to Germany was the climax for Herzl of years of wrestling intellectually with the problem of Jew-hatred. According to Herzl, then the Paris correspondent of the *Neue Freie Presse,* the Dreyfus affair "embodies the desire of the vast majority of the French to condemn a Jew, and to condemn all Jews in this one Jew. Death to the Jews! howled the mob, as the decorations were being ripped from the captain's coat . . ." [2] If France, the first European power to emancipate its Jews, could so behave, it appeared well-nigh impossible to hope for the complete acceptance of the Jew into Western society.

Within weeks of that experience, Herzl had sketched out rough plans for a solution: the organization and training of the Jewish people for migration to their own land. In 1896 his book *Der Judenstaat* ("The Jewish State") appeared. Starting from the premise that anti-Semitism was ineradicable as long as the majority of Jews lived outside their own homeland, it spelled out the political, economic, and technical efforts necessary for the creation of a state, as well as the functions that a democratic Jewish commonwealth should perform. Herzl called for a world Zionist congress to be held in August 1897 in Basel, Switzerland, and over two hundred delegates from all over the world, including one from the United States, responded. Despite the opposition of assimilated Western Jews to a project which belied their periodic protests that Judaism was no more than a religion, the congress drew up a platform which guided the Zionist movement for the next fifty years. The Basel Program read:

> Zionism seeks to create for the Jewish people a home in Palestine secured by public law. The Congress contemplates the following means to the attainment of this end:
> 1. The promotion by appropriate means of the settlement in Palestine of Jewish agriculturalists, artisans and manufacturers.
> 2. The organization and binding together of the whole of Jewry by means of appropriate institutions, both local and international, in accordance with the laws of each country.
> 3. The strengthening and fostering of Jewish national sentiment and national consciousness.
> 4. Preparatory steps toward obtaining the consent of governments, where necessary, in order to reach the goal of Zionism. [3]

The congress also established a World Zionist Organization under Herzl's presidency, and adopted a national anthem and flag. Symbols were important according to Herzl. "With a flag," he said, "people are led—perhaps even to the Promised Land." [4]

Herzl's detailed blueprint of a Jewish state was novel, but the dream of a national life in Palestine was not. Although *Zionism* and *Zionist* were terms which became current only in the 1890s, a return to Zion and a renewal of independent statehood had been central to Jewish eschatological thought ever since the destruction of the Temple by the Romans in the first century. Throughout the ages pious individuals had journeyed to Palestine to live a fuller religious life and to hasten the coming of the messiah.

Poets, novelists, and even pseudomessiahs had invoked national imagery for artistic and political purposes. Some strands of Christian religious thought also espoused a Jewish return to Palestine, for many non-Jews believed that restoration was a precondition to the second coming of Jesus.

In the modern era, when the Enlightenment ideals of individual rights and universal brotherhood held sway in Western Europe, large numbers of Jews were prepared and even eager to scrap their religious-national sentiments, along with other so-called archaic beliefs, for the sake of emancipation and acceptance into society. Assimilation made rapid strides within the Western Jewish communities: modern schools were set up; synagogue services were revamped to make room for the organ, the sermon, and the use of the vernacular. Some Jews, including the poet Heinrich Heine, even paid the ultimate price, conversion to Christianity. Clearly, if conversion was the mandatory passport to social acceptance, the Enlightenment ideals had faded. The resulting disappointment in the West and the total frustration in the East, where universalist goals were never more than fantasies for the Jewish masses, were compounded by the deterioration of the framework of Jewish existence. Even where physical separatism still obtained, new intellectual currents of politics, economics, science, and education were destroying the foundations of age-old community authority. His faith shaken, the Jew could no longer find his emotional security within the traditionally self-contained and insulated Jewish community. Many were caught stranded, their bridge to the past burned and the gateway to the modern world blocked.

After 1860 Jewish thinkers took up once more the theme of national restoration. They drew upon the nationalist capital of the religious heritage, but as modern men they couched their ideas in nonreligious terms which mirrored the realities of nineteenth-century European nationalism and modern anti-Semitism.

That new ideology was attuned particularly to the needs of the Russian Jews. Dislodged from their traditional economic roles as artisans and small entrepreneurs by the inroads of capitalism, and increasingly the target for persecution and physical violence by a government and church dedicated to autocracy and Russification, the Jews despaired of a future under the tsar. Assimilation that stopped short of conversion was not encouraged by a hostile society. Although many Jews were in revolt against Orthodoxy and traditional education, the reformulation of Judaism into a universalist religious creed was alien to their shtetl upbringing, and, without the anticipated reward of emancipation, utterly meaningless. Many turned to emigration—to Western Europe, to the New World; some, imbued with the vision of socialism, joined the revolutionary movement. These solutions did not preclude Zionist sympathies, but Palestine as an immediate practical alternative attracted only a small number. The country was backward, the land itself poor and disease-ridden. It was ruled by arbitrary Turkish officials, masters of the art of baksheesh, who suspected Europeans generally and Russians in particular; while the old existent Jewish communities, supported by the alms collected from coreligionists all over the world, resisted any disruption of their ghettoized way of life. Nevertheless, a movement of Russian Jews, many of them secularized students, dedicated itself to the building of a new society on Palestinian soil. Known as the Lovers of Zion, these pioneers founded about twenty agricultural colonies during the last two decades of the nineteenth century. Although the extreme hardships they faced and the tragic failures they sustained prevented a migration of major proportions, the new settlements heralded the creation of a modern, secularist life-style in the ancient and holy land.

Herzl, a Western Jew who knew little of Jewish culture and did not share the tradition-nurtured attachment to Zion, was unaware in 1896 of the work of his East European predecessors. But he succeeded in guiding that nascent Zionism in new directions. He disapproved of piecemeal colonization efforts, insisting that Jews first gain legal, internationally recognized rights to Palestine. He personally sought access to heads of state, for, he said, a Jewish state could and would come into being only with the cooperation of the world powers. Zionism thus became a political movement within world politics, another element to be weighed in the calculations of realpolitik. Herzl also made Zionism a mass movement. Failing to elicit the support of the powerful Jewish philanthropists, Maurice de Hirsch and Edmond de Rothschild, he harnessed his goals to a broad popular base, making Zionism dependent upon the participation and contributions of Jews throughout the world. Above all, he infused the Zionist ideal with dedicated and enthusiastic leadership. Visionary and romantic—some even called him an egomaniac—he saw himself as the leader of a historic mission. He died in 1904 at the age of forty-four, but despite the brief duration of his leadership, his magnetic personality and his faith in the inevitability of Jewish statehood combined to fire the loyalty of countless Jews.

The Zionist movement refused to die with Herzl, and in 1917 the Balfour Declaration stamped the founder's dream with the seal of international respectability. The Jewish state was born some thirty years later in the grim aftermath of the Nazi Holocaust. From the War of Independence in 1948 until 1967, Israel led an uneasy existence, twice more taking up arms against its Arab neighbors to assert its legitimacy as a nation. Within that half century (1917–67) of political turmoil, two world wars, and changing global alignments, a new civilization was developing on Palestinian soil. The immigrants to Zion, most of East European origin, experimented with different forms of social organization. The culture they fashioned drew little from the Levantine surroundings or pre-Zionist Jewish settlements. Rather they created an outpost of Western thought and technology in what was essentially a premodern area of the world. In that new society their children, the native prickly sabras, never experienced the shock of displacement or alienation from the majority. Unlike their forefathers they were at home.

Seven thousand miles away much the same process was at work within the American Jewish community. By 1917, on the eve of America's entry into World War I, that community had been stamped indelibly by the two million East European immigrants who had arrived since 1870. Jews had lived in the United States ever since the *St. Charles* landed at New Amsterdam in 1654, but the East Europeans ultimately contributed a new dimension to the emerging modern American Jewish life. While acclimatizing rapidly to the new environment, they were never absorbed into the Jewish mold of the Spanish or German Jews who had preceded them. Their social, religious, and communal patterns supplemented those of their predecessors. By 1967, overwhelmingly native-born and virtually unscathed by anti-Semitism, they were rooted in the United States, where, in numbers and affluence, their community surpassed all others in Jewish history.

Ties of kinship as well as parallels in social development linked the Palestinian settlement with that of twentieth-century American Jewry. Both sprang from the same European roots, in many cases drawing immigrants from the same villages and the same families. Like branches of one river, both streams drew intellectual sustenance from their ethnic heritage and from the currents of secularist thought. Both aimed for the liberation and self-fulfillment of the individual and the group, and both defined liberation to include a break with traditional Judaism and its East European ghetto life-style. The Zionist tilled the soil of the Holy Land and spoke the Holy Tongue, but even those who were not militantly antireligious discarded traditions which could not be imbued with nationalist meaning. The American Jew, intoxicated by the voluntaristic character of religion in the United

States, eclectically chose random elements from his heritage to form an amalgam that served his emotional needs and was compatible with his secularist surroundings. He and the Zionist refused to adhere to the pattern of the passive, long-suffering Jew who waited for divine salvation. Each claimed an active role in building a new life in a secular promised land. Together they ultimately supplanted Eastern Europe, making America and Palestine the geographical and spiritual centers of Jewish life.

From 1917 through 1967 American Jews poured money, political influence, and even manpower into the creation and maintenance of a Jewish state. Their contributions were often crucial, at times dramatic, and they added up to an unprecedented philanthropic achievement. The deeper question of why they responded in the way they did is the focus of this study. On one level that response was a byproduct of other circumstances —particularly the needs of European Jewry. In large measure it was determined by the degree of Jewish affluence and security. It also reflected the views of government and society on Zionism and on ethnic loyalties generally, for as a small minority with a long history of persecution, Jews were understandably sensitive to the opinions of their host country. On another level, Zionism was more than a fixed quantity to be responded to, independent of the American Jewish experience. It was, in fact, a vital component in the internal development of American Judaism. Just as Zionism needed the support of American Jewry, so did the latter need Zionism in charting a viable course between the antagonistic poles of assimilation within the majority and survival of the minority group. For American Jews, Zionism primarily signified an affirmation of Jewish "groupness"—an acceptance of a common tradition, history, and fate—rather than an implied personal commitment to another land. It stimulated new forms of cultural and religious expression as well as new communal institutions; it generated a new image of the Jew within the Jewish and non-Jewish communities. Most important, it offered a solution to the fundamental question with which Jews had grappled since the collapse of the ghetto: how to survive as a Jew in the free nation-state. A product of acculturation, American Zionism from 1917 to 1967 reflected the maturation of the Jewish community in the United States. It testified also to the course of assimilation on the part of a religious-ethnic minority within a pluralistic society. In short, American Jewish interest in a Jewish homeland has been the product of the American environment no less than of the Jewish heritage.

1

A Pattern Is Set

I

When Herzl's message reached the United States it was not alien in sound. America had its own sentimental ties with Zion dating back to the Puritans, who, as the self-styled Children of Israel, strove to build a new Promised Land in the wilderness. The names they gave their children and their settlements, the laws they wrote into their codes, testified to their familiarity and sympathy with biblical themes. Religious fundamentalism and romantic currents in the nineteenth century moved some American Christians, like some Christians in Europe, to favor the restoration of the Jews to Palestine. A few even embarked on projects of their own to settle that land.

Within the American Jewish community links with Palestine had always existed. Since colonial times emissaries from Palestine had been arriving periodically to collect funds for the support of the Jewish community. Like Jews all over the world, American Jews faced east when they prayed, and their prayerbooks contained numerous references to Zion. Some insisted on being interred with a handful of Palestinian soil; Commodore Uriah P. Levy, the first Jew to obtain high rank in the U.S. Navy, brought a wagonload of such earth to the United States aboard an American warship. There were also a few individuals who foreshadowed Zionist settlement of Palestine: Mordecai Manuel Noah, minor politician and diplomat, who saw the need for human efforts to effect a restoration to Zion; Warder Cresson, an affluent religious mystic, who converted to Judaism and as Michael Boaz Israel began an agricultural settlement near Jerusalem; Simon Bermann, who, after seventeen years in the United States, moved to Palestine where he designed plans for an agricultural cooperative; the poetess Emma Lazarus, who, under the influence of Jewish nationalist

Leo Pinsker and of England's Lawrence Oliphant and George Eliot, advanced the ideal of restoration in "epistles" to American Jewry. American Jews also had their "Lovers of Zion" movement, which stressed the practical advantages of small-scale colonization in Palestine.

On occasion even American heads of state took note of restoration projects. President John Adams made the following comment on Noah's ideas: "I really wish the Jews again in Judaea, an independent nation." [1] Anticipating Herzl on anti-Semitism, Thomas Jefferson also agreed with Noah: "For altho' we are free by the law, we are not so in practice. . . . the prejudices still scowling on your section of our religion . . . cannot be unfelt by yourselves." [2]

America's concrete involvement in Palestinian matters, dating from the establishment of a consular district for Jerusalem in 1856, was minimal. At times the consuls were called upon to protect the civil rights of Jews who had been naturalized in the United States and to settle American Jewish claims to share in the *halukah* (charity system), which supported the non-laboring religious groupings in Palestine. In the last two decades of the nineteenth century the government was alerted to the possibility of Palestine's being used as a haven for Russian Jewish victims of pogroms and economic strangulation. General Lewis Wallace, American minister to Constantinople in 1882, secured the administration's consent for his support of Jewish colonies. In 1891 the Blackstone Memorial, signed by over four hundred prominent Americans, called for the return of Palestine to the Jews. Asking the president to confer with the world powers on the plight of the Jews and their claims to Palestine, it prompted the State Department to inquire whether Turkey might be amenable to considering such plans. The State Department, and the Sublime Porte as well, was also kept aware of Jewish interests in Palestine by an American Jew, Oscar S. Straus, who served as minister to Constantinople from 1887 to 1889 and from 1898 to 1900. Straus was officially concerned only with the rights of Americans, but on several occasions he acted as a champion of general Jewish immigration and settlement. He dismissed the Zionist program as chimerical, but he suggested to Secretary John Hay that perhaps Turkey could be persuaded to permit Jews to settle in Mesopotamia. The United States had not yet emerged as a world power with distinctive economic and strategic interests in the Near East. But since the government was committed to the protection of the powerful missionary interests in the Ottoman Empire, their needs dictated caution in dealing with Turkey. In 1899 Hay doubtless thought first of the pending missionary claims for damages suffered in the wake of the Armenian massacres when he agreed to Turkish restriction of American Jewish immigration.

Before World War I the government paid scant attention to political Zionism. At home the dominant theme was reform according to progressive goals: regulation of the economy in the public interest, extension of public participation in the democratic process, formulation of social-welfare measures to ameliorate the economic plight of the lower classes. In the area of international affairs the country was staking out its first serious claims to political and economic control in Latin America and the Far East.

Americans who expressed opinions of political Zionism at first ignored the diplomatic implications of the movement. Some religious spokesmen responded enthusiastically, seeing the restoration of a Jewish Palestine as a forerunner of mass conversion to Christianity. Other Americans, loyal to the canons of their progressive ideas, applauded the planning and experimental emphasis—both agricultural and social—of the Zionist movement. Still others criticized what they considered Jewish separatism and the implication that American Jews could have other national sentiments in addition to their Americanism.

Opposition to Zionism crystallized when dollar diplomacy, or the government's drive for economic concessions for American firms in foreign countries, was promoted seriously. Since the Ottoman Empire was a potential field for investment, some businessmen viewed Zionism as an obstacle in the path of cultivating Turkish goodwill. Their objections were reinforced when the missionaries realized that the Jews in Palestine were unlikely converts, that as products and examples of modern secular forces they actually hindered the progress of religious missionizing. Catering to the Muslim population, the missionaries became identified with the Arabs' nationalist cause.

But just as the business-missionary alliance gave rise to a tradition of anti-Zionism, which was consistently to pervade the bureaucratic levels of government, other patterns that emerged before World War I checked the government's proclivity to an unswerving anti-Zionist posture. First of all, the recurring pogroms in Russia in the early 1900s gave added justification to the movement for a safe homeland. With each new crisis American Jews and non-Jews grew more accustomed to interpreting the value of Zionism in terms of physical survival. Secondly, by 1914 large numbers of East European Jews in the United States had become Americanized sufficiently to articulate their demands and register their opinions through the ballot box. Increasingly sympathetic to Zionism, even if not enrolled in Zionist organizations, they eventually made it an ever-present issue in American domestic politics.

II

At first, Herzl's book and the organization of the world Zionist movement mustered only feeble support within the American Jewish community. That community was then in a state of flux. Its numbers were being augmented annually by the scores of thousands as more and more East Europeans made their way to the New World. From 1880 until 1914 Jewish immigrants totaled about two million, eight times the number of all American Jews in 1880. Some were Zionists when they came; others were socialists or cultural nationalists. Secularist or religious, most were strongly imbued with the sense of ethnic solidarity. Nevertheless, the new arrivals, who had opted for a haven of refuge in the United States, desired first and foremost to become Americans, to enjoy the benefits of political freedom and economic opportunity which the promise of America held out. Their concerns were personal: to find a place economically, socially, emotionally within a strange environment. Their energies focused on immediate problems of tenement living, factory labor, the rescue of relatives from tsarist oppression. Their social and cultural institutions—synagogues, newspapers, *landsmanschaften* and charities—developed rapidly and served as agencies both of cohesiveness and of Americanization.

After World War I, through sheer force of numbers, the East Europeans progressively displaced the older Jewish leadership and stamped American Judaism with their own imprint. When they first arrived, the Jewish "establishment" consisted of Jews of German origin, whose families had immigrated a generation earlier, and who were of the upper-middle class and Reform in synagogue affiliation. Classical Reform, in essence, was the antithesis of Zionism. It excised the idea of a return to Zion from its ritual and prayers and substituted the concept of a Jewish mission to teach the peoples of the world the prophetic code of social ethics. A product of Enlightenment optimism and universalism, Reform flowered in the United States, where leaders like Rabbi Isaac Mayer Wise stressed the similarities between Reform values and the American promise. Since it sanctioned assimilation in order to attain full political liberty for Western Jews, Reform proceeded to divest Judaism of most of its ethnic and particularistic trappings. Judaism was no more than a religion; Jews had only one national allegiance, and that was to the land in which they lived.

By the 1880s it appeared that the future of American Judaism lay with Reform. Vibrant and dynamic, it was the first Jewish religious movement in the United States to unify its following through an organization of congregations (Union of American Hebrew Congregations, 1873), an organization of rabbis (Central Conference of American Rabbis, 1889), and a rabbinical seminary (Hebrew Union College, 1875). In 1881 over fifty percent of the major American congregations were affiliated with Reform institutions. The spokesmen of the Jewish community, usually laymen rather than rabbis, were members of those congregations. Reform Jews were an urban middle-class group and highly Americanized. Only a different style of worship and a marked sense of responsibility to other Jews set them apart from their fellow Americans.

The German Jews had created a maze of secular agencies to perform functions originally associated with the pre-Emancipation European synagogue. They set up hospitals and orphanages, fraternal lodges and "Y"s, and social and cultural groups. Going further afield, they founded the Jewish Publication Society and several years later the American Jewish Historical Society. In 1906 they organized the small but influential American Jewish Committee, dedicated to the defense of Jewish rights in the United States and abroad. B'nai B'rith's defense arm, the Anti-Defamation League, followed in 1913.

Even before the appearance of defense organizations, the established Jewish community looked beyond its own comfortable circumstances and assumed responsibility for ameliorating the plight of foreign Jews. Despite their antinationalist convictions and assimilationist bent, the Jewish leaders steadfastly adhered to the traditional ideal of communal stewardship. They, the ones who enjoyed high economic and social status, felt obligated to render service to their less fortunate brethren. From the turn of the century until World War I they concentrated on keeping America's doors open to immigrants in the face of mounting restrictionist sentiment, on aiding the new immigrants to adjust to American society, and on galvanizing popular and governmental opposition to the persecution of Jews in Eastern Europe. These self-imposed tasks kept alive a spirit of group kinship which transcended strictly religious loyalties. Dissimilarities in language, culture, and outlook sharply separated the established community from the new immigrants, but philanthropy, practiced on a steward-ward pattern, was the first link which would weld the two groups together.

Reform led the American Jewish opposition to Herzlian Zionism. From pulpit, press, and organization, rabbis and laymen denounced the movement in unequivocal terms. The statement of the Union of American Hebrew Congregations in 1898 was typical:

> We are unalterably opposed to political Zionism. The Jews are not a nation, but a religious community. Zion was a precious possession of the past, the early home of our faith, where our prophets uttered their world-subduing thoughts, and our psalmists sang their world-enchanting hymns. As such it is a holy memory, but it is not our hope of the future. America is our Zion. Here, in the home of religious liberty, we have aided in founding this new Zion, the fruition of the beginning laid in the old. The mission of Judaism is spiritual, not political. Its aim is not to establish a state, but to spread the truths of religion and humanity throughout the world. [3]

Not only did Zionism represent to these critics a regression from the universalist principles of Reform theology, but, as an import of East European origin, it conflicted with the Reform goals of assimilation and deghettoization. Reform leaders, in tune with general public opinion, believed that the immigrant must be divested of his cultural baggage and made to conform to American patterns as set by the Anglo-Saxon stock. Zionism also raised the specter of dual political loyalties, which, Reform argued, would cast doubts upon the patriotism of diaspora Jews and lend credence to the charges of anti-Semites. Since the success of Zionism depended upon international recognition and the amassing of large amounts of capital, Reform called the movement impractical and ridiculed its leaders as shallow opportunists. Reform leaders were always ready to entertain plans for ameliorating the situation of.the East European Jew, but Zionism—colonization or mass immigration into Palestine—was never considered seriously. Indeed, territorialism, a movement to find a haven for the East Europeans in some relatively unpopulated area outside Palestine, appealed to some as eminently more practical. Tending to minimize the significance of American anti-Semitism, Reform denied that Zionism served any purpose for American Jews. Kaufmann Kohler, a leading Reform theologian, summed up the dominant opinion as follows: "If anti-Semitism sets the brain of Herzl on fire, must we act as madmen too?" [4] When Reform spokesmen intoned the phrase "America is our Zion and Washington our Jerusalem," they were affirming a theological tenet, a political sentiment, and a faith regarding their personal security in the United States.

Others within the Jewish community added criticisms of Zionism on different grounds. Orthodox Jews opposed a restoration contrived by man because it ignored the traditional belief in the role of a divinely commissioned messiah. They also objected to the secular and areligious cast of the Zionist movement. Jewish socialists of the purist stripe rejected Jewish nationalism, like all other nationalisms, in favor of class loyalty. A national conference of Jewish labor organizations held in New York in 1890 expressed its universalist outlook in the motto, "The world is our fatherland, socialism is our religion." [5] Jewish socialists harnessed their energies to the development of trade unionism, and at the beginning, some even interpreted Zionism as an antilabor weapon of the capitalist class. However, since Reform was the most influential and articulate element, it reached the widest audiences. Abetted by the leading Anglo-Jewish periodicals, it even contributed to the development of non-Jewish opposition to Zionism.

Despite the obstacles posed by a culturally and ideologically divided community, the problems of the new immigrants, and the strong voice of Jewish critics, Zionism took root in American society. Though all Zionists pledged fealty to the goals of the Basel Platform, they differed on questions of religious and economic philosophy. The three most important societies reflecting the basic ideological divisions came into being before the outbreak of World War I: Federation of American Zionists (FAZ), the general Herzlian wing, in 1898; Mizrachi, the religious wing, in 1903; Poale Zion, the labor wing, in 1905. Hadassah, a women's organization which steered clear of politics and concentrated on health projects in Palestine, was born in 1912. Like Zionists all over the world, Americans paid their shekel, or annual dues, and sent delegates to the World Zionist Congresses. They kept in close touch with the Zionist leadership in Europe, and the latter in turn sent emissaries to the United States to reinforce the efforts within the young community. The organizations pledged themselves to the support of Jewish education in the United States, but in reality Zionism on the American scene redounded principally to propaganda work and fundraising.[6]

While the labor and religious groups were almost solely East European from top to bottom, the FAZ drew upon the Americanized stratum of the Jewish community for its leadership. Men like Gustav and Richard Gottheil, Bernhard Felsenthal, Stephen S. Wise, and Judah Magnes proved that not all "established" Jews or even Reform rabbis were antagonistic to the Zionist message. Sensitive to the suffering in East Europe and the resurgence of political anti-Semitism in West Europe, they could not throw off their belief in Jewish peoplehood. Some attended the early Zionist Congresses, where they were captivated by Herzl's charisma and by the spirit of union with Jews from other countries. Stephen Wise explained his conversion at the Second Zionist Congress:

> Suddenly, and as if by magic, I came upon a company of Jews who were not victims, nor refugees, nor beggars, but proud and educated men, dreaming, planning, toiling for their people. . . . Thrilled and grateful, I caught a first glimpse of the power and pride and the nobleness of the Jewish people, which my American upbringing and even service to New York Jewry had not in any degree given me. [7]

Wise saw Zionism as a means of infusing new life into American Judaism; others believed it would develop the new Jew—the Jew who by self-help would live a normal life like other peoples. The main contribution of such men was to translate the meaning of Zionism to the English-speaking public. By virtue of their own position in American society they also succeeded in making Zionism more respectable and less foreign in the eyes of the Jewish upper class as well as more appealing to the new immigrants. In the long run, the fact that the Americanized Jews met the new immigrants under Zionist banners helped to unite the American Jewish community.

Richard Gottheil, professor of Semitics at Columbia University, was the first president of the FAZ, but his two younger associates, Wise and Magnes, became more famous in the annals of American Zionism. Stephen Wise, the founder and rabbi of the Free Synagogue, was a liberal in theology. Prophet rather than priest, he was primarily a crusader against social ills, a reformer who fought on the side of the NAACP, women's suffrage, improvement of working conditions, pacifism, clean city government. A tall, impressive figure and a gifted orator who could convey his passion through the spoken word, he captivated audiences in synagogues and lecture halls throughout the country. His favorite cause was Zionism, and his friendships with many prominent non-Jews, as well as his association with the Democratic party, were often employed on behalf of the Jewish nationalist movement. During the 1930s and World War II, he took a leading part in mounting public demonstrations on behalf of Jewish victims of nazism. Wise always idealized Herzl, and he was fond of recounting how Herzl had told him privately that he, Wise, would live to see a Jewish state. Wise did; he died in 1949 shortly after the establishment of Israel.

If Wise was frequently the independent who would not curb his zeal to conform to organizational discipline, Judah Magnes was even more the uncompromising maverick. A native American, Magnes was raised in California and ordained at the Reform seminary in Cincinnati. His appointment as rabbi of New York's prestigious Temple Emanu-El and his connection by marriage to the Louis Marshall family eased him naturally into the German Jewish establishment. But Magnes interpreted his role to include ministering to the entire community. He learned Yiddish in order to work with the new immigrants, and he captured their attention by leading a movement which advocated armed self-defense for East European Jews threatened by pogroms To the immigrants the young, handsome rabbi was a modern Maccabee. Magnes's most ambitious aim was to forge a vibrant Jewish community through the creation of a democratic Kehillah.[8] His dedication and leadership contributed to the Kehillah's initial successes, but the venture died with World War I. At the same time Magnes was repudiating the antinationalist teachings of Reform and preaching cultural Zionism. He even attempted a "counter-reformation," a way of making Reform more traditional, but he eventually left the rabbinate because he could not carry his congregation with him. Disillusioned by the politics of the American Zionist organization during the war, and personally out of favor for having remained true to his pacifist convictions, Magnes was left with his love for Palestine. He had long been identified with the plan to erect a Hebrew University in Jerusalem, and when that institution was opened in 1925 he became its chancellor—one of the first American pioneers to settle in Palestine.

Despite the endorsement by these well-known personalities, the FAZ counted fewer than fifteen thousand members in 1914. Plagued by lack of funds and the disunity attendant upon a federation-type structure, it was also weakened by the socioeconomic chasm between the Americanized leaders and the Yiddish-speaking poorer members. A positive stimulus for the organization's growth came in 1906, when Solomon Schechter publicly endorsed Zionism.

An erudite and secularly trained authority on rabbinics who was also a vibrant personality, Schechter had been brought to the United States to head the Jewish Theological Seminary. His sponsors, although Reform in their personal affiliations, knew that the East European immigrants could be reached and Americanized by leaders more closely identified with traditional Judaism. Rumanian-born Schechter became the prime mover in developing the ideology of Conservative Judaism, a movement committed to the preservation of historical Judaism within the framework of modern scholarship and thought. Schechter viewed Judaism as a culture as well as a religion. Zionism to him was primarily a check to assimilation. He believed that the rays emanating from a Jewish center in Palestine would infuse religious and cultural vitality into Judaism wherever it existed.

> Zionism declares boldly to the world that Judaism means to preserve its life by *not* losing its life. It shall be a true and healthy life, with a policy of its own, a religion wholly its own, invigorated by sacred memories and sacred environments, and proving a tower of strength and of unity not only for the remnant gathered within the borders of the Holy Land, but also for those who shall, by choice or necessity, prefer what now constitutes the Galut.[9]

Schechter and his faculty transmitted the teachings of cultural Zionism to a generation of Seminary-trained rabbis and through them to their congregations. Ultimately, Conservative Judaism became the most Zionist-oriented religious grouping of American Jews.

Not all contributions to the upbuilding of Palestine came from the ranks of organized Zionists. Even in this early period some who called themselves anti-Zionists or non-Zionists supported practical work in the land connected with specific institutions. For example, Jacob Schiff and Louis Marshall, outstanding communal leaders, spoke out against the Herzlian movement but actively aided in the establishment of a technical institute at Haifa and agricultural experimental stations throughout Palestine. Far different was the commitment made by individuals to settle on the land despite the physical hardships and the recurrent failures of similar experiments. The plan for aliyah on the part of a dozen agricultural students in New Jersey deserves mention, for the experiences of that group ultimately led to the establishment of the first cooperative smallholders' settlement (*moshav ovdim*) in Palestine. Another American attempt at colonization was the *achuza* idea, whereby groups of Jews planning to settle in Palestine invested in newly staked-out plantations for several years before immigrating. In this way they provided the necessary capital for the initial period; they themselves would arrive in Palestine when their plantations were ready to yield fruit. By 1913 there were seven *achuza* groups in the United States, but the outbreak of World War I cut short the development of the three settlements which had taken root in Palestine.

III

Despite the weakness of the movement in the prewar period, a foundation was laid for American Zionism which was to distinguish it radically from its East European counterpart. For the East European, Zionism was more relevant personally. It filled cultural, nationalist, and emotional needs, especially for the Jew who was unwelcome in the larger society. Not too different from the nationalist aspirations of other ethnic groups who were his neighbors in Eastern Europe, it also held out the promise of a haven of refuge which he himself might conceivably require. The average American, on the other hand, unexposed to currents of minority nationalism and secure in his political rights, viewed Zionism primarily as a philanthropic ideal for the benefit of others. Emma Lazarus's *Epistle to the Hebrews,* one of the first propaganda leaflets issued by the FAZ, summarized that point of view:

> There is not the slightest necessity for an American Jew, the free citizen of a republic, to rest his hopes upon the foundation of any other nationality soever, or to decide whether he individually would or would not be in favor of residing in Palestine. All that would be claimed from him would be a patriotic and unselfish interest in the suffering of his oppressed brethren of less fortunate countries, sufficient to make him promote by every means in his power the establishment of a secure asylum.[10]

Even Herzl phrased his call to American Jews in terms of remembering their unfortunate brethren abroad. For all practical purposes, Palestine was conceived of as a refuge built by a vanguard of a few pioneering Jews, supported by the wealthy, but peopled largely by refugees. American Zionism affirmed a messianic goal, not unlike the messianism of the early American restorationists, but it did not exact a personal commitment to settle in Palestine. When men like Solomon Schechter interpreted Zionism as a means for providing a strongly religious national life for diaspora Jewry as well as for those in Palestine, they found the formula for reconciling Zionism and Americanism.

American Zionists never faced up to the inconsistencies of their position. To maintain that they could indeed build a strong religious-national life in the diaspora and were absolved from the need of living in Palestine, belied their acceptance of Herzl's position on anti-Semitism. Like Herzl, the early American Zionists despaired of the Jew ever attaining true equality. Even in countries where no legal disabilities existed, the Jew was not really accepted into society. Nevertheless, they stopped short of predicting doom for the Jewish future in America. They reconciled Zionism and their faith in America by positing a fixed axiom: the United States was different. Usually unspoken, that premise became the cornerstone of American Zionist ideology.

In that way the American Zionists could enjoy both their American world and their Jewish ethnic world. They took great pride in Jewish peoplehood. Assimilation was contemptible, a cowardly and suicidal act on the part of a people. Zionism would preserve Jewish culture and "virtues." In Judah Magnes's words, a race needed a homeland in order to express its genius. Even if the American Jew was not dependent upon Zionism for his physical security, his status in the diaspora would be enhanced by the existence of a Jewish state. More important, he would enjoy greater self-confidence, self-reliance, courage, and nobility of spirit—all of which derived from a heightened national pride.

At the same time that they preached Jewish nationalism, Zionists constantly fought the charge that their beliefs in any way made them less loyal to America. Logically, this would lead them to support cultural pluralism in place of the melting-pot theory of Americanization, and, indeed, Magnes broached that theme as early as 1909. Those very efforts proved that Zionists never entertained the thought of disengagement from the American scene. The *Maccabaean,* the journal of the FAZ, combatted anti-Semitism and argued for the separation of church and state, thus laboring to make Jewish life in the United States more secure. Early Zionists also abstained from mixing Zionist interests with American politics. Richard Gottheil unequivocally rejected a suggestion that Zionists come out for McKinley in 1900 if the president promised them his support.[11] That too reflected the efforts of a still insecure minority not to incur the displeasure of their fellow Americans. Eager to be part of the larger society and to show the affinity of Jewish nationalism with American values, Zionists drew parallels between their goals and those of the American Puritans.

Although they saw their own future in the United States, the early Zionists did not form a distinct grouping or join alignments within the American political spectrum. Nor did they offer any comprehensive program for the development and perpetuation of an American Jewish community life. To construct that kind of program would have been daring, radical, and, given the unsettled conditions of the immigrant population, probably premature. By attempting to hold on to both worlds without defining reasons or methods, the FAZ, the major Zionist organization, never developed the force or appeal of an ideological crusade. Nevertheless, the same omissions and ambiguities enabled it to bring together individuals with different interpretations of Zionism in a common effort to build a Jewish state. Its ideological shortcomings also made American Zionism inoffensive to most non-Jews. They saw it as a philanthropic endeavor on behalf of persecuted European Jews or as a reformist movement, akin to those they themselves engaged in, to enlarge the area of freedom for greater numbers. In an era when the interest of the United States in world affairs was increasing, Zionism matched that current of thought which emphasized humanitarian and idealistic reasons for American involvement abroad.

American Zionism in its early years contributed to the maturation of the Jewish community in two ways. Americans who attended the Zionist Congresses and participated in the decision-making process added status to American Jewry in the eyes of their European coreligionists. They forged another link in the ties binding the Jewries of both continents, and they strengthened the voice of American Jews in the management of general Jewish affairs. Secondly, American Zionists spearheaded the move to extend democracy within their own community. Stemming from Zionism's appeal to the rank and file, that move was in tune with the democratic cast of progressive ideology. It found a receptive audience because the American Zionist following came largely from the lower socioeconomic strata of society and its opposition from the upper stratum. Zionist leaders roundly criticized the American Jewish stewards and the unrepresentative organizations for presuming to speak for the Jewish masses. Attacking "benevolent despotism," they insisted that freedom and self-help replace charity. Such teachings evoked self-assertiveness on the part of the new immigrants and, ultimately, furthered independence from the control of the oligarchic Jewish establishment.

2

Zionism as Progressivism

I

Just as World War I thrust the United States into a role of world leadership, so did it affect American Zionists. The World Zionist Executive, its headquarters in Berlin, could no longer maintain contact with members in outlying states. In August 1914 a conference was called of the major American Zionist groups. It resulted in the creation of the Provisional Executive Committee for General Zionist Affairs, which was to assume the functions of the Berlin office: the support of Zionist institutions in Palestine and the direction of Zionist propaganda.

Fortunately for the cause of Zionism, the transference of leadership coincided with the Zionist "conversion" of Louis Dembitz Brandeis. Brandeis, who was elected chairman of the Provisional Executive Committee, was first and foremost a liberal, a man who fused the creed of European liberalism with the American faith in democracy. His parents had emigrated from Bohemia along with others who sought refuge in the United States upon the collapse of the democratic goals of the 1848 revolution. They settled in the slave state of Kentucky, where they identified with the abolitionist cause and where their son, Louis David, was born in 1856. As a growing lad he was influenced by his maternal uncle, Louis Dembitz, whose name he added to his own. Dembitz was a prominent and learned Jew in the community and a Republican lawyer who worked for the election of Lincoln. The tradition of liberalism, both in politics and religion, that Brandeis imbibed was reinforced by his marriage to the daughter of Joseph Goldmark, a well-known German Jewish Forty-eighter and a distant relative. Like others of that mold, Brandeis received only sketchy training in Judaism. He never shrank from or disavowed his Jewishness, but his consciousness as a Jew lay dormant.

14

Brandeis completed his education at Harvard Law School, where he set an unprecedented scholastic record. He found his métier in the intellectual circles of Boston and decided to make his home there. His tastes, behavior, and moral code led one observer to call him "a Puritan in spirit and conduct." [1] From the time he left a comfortable practice in corporate law to fight social issues through litigation, Brandeis became part of the history of American progressivism. The "people's attorney," an architect of sociological jurisprudence, and a distinguished jurist on the nation's highest court, he wielded great influence in reformist circles. He served as trusted adviser to Woodrow Wilson, whose New Freedom policies owed much to Brandeis's direction, and his philosophy underlay a good deal of Franklin Roosevelt's domestic program. It was Roosevelt who referred to Brandeis as "Isaiah."

Brandeis had shown scant interest in or knowledge of Jewish issues before he negotiated the settlement of the cloakmakers' strike of 1910. Only then did he come into contact with the way of life of the East European Jewish immigrants. Shortly thereafter he espoused the Zionist cause, a result attributed principally to the influence of Jacob De Haas. The close friendship of the two men was a study in contrasts. Whereas Brandeis typified the rational intellectual, the lucid analyst, the man who amassed specifics to buttress a well-reasoned case, De Haas was a romantic, a dreamer, an imaginative raconteur. A journalist in London, he had attended the First Zionist Congress, where he fell under Herzl's spell. He worked closely with Herzl, whom he idolized as the one to redeem the Jews through the Zionist movement, and it was Herzl who sent him to the United States to assist in the activities of the FAZ. De Haas left the organization after a few years and went to Boston, where he edited a Jewish newspaper. There he met Brandeis and, so the story goes, educated him in the course of private conversations with respect to the needs of the Jews and the ideals of Zionism and of Herzl in particular. In Brandeis, De Haas found a second hero, a worthy successor to Theodor Herzl.

Brandeis came to Zionism when he was over fifty years old, and his new loyalty signified an awakening of his ethnic consciousness. But his commitment to the movement did not stem from an identification with the cultural heritage and history of East European Jewry, which were the bricks and mortar of Zionism. He did not grasp the subtle differences in ideology among European Zionists, nor did he have patience with their interminable theoretical discussions. Rather, he fit Zionism into his already articulated liberal, reformist, American creed.

To Brandeis Zionism was American and progressive even more than it was Jewish. In fact he saw the preservation of a Jewish national group as serving certain universalist needs. In his speech accepting the office of chairman he said:

> I find Jews possessed of those very qualities which we of the twentieth century seek to develop in our struggle for justice and democracy; a deep moral feeling which makes them capable of noble acts; a deep sense of the brotherhood of man; and a high intelligence, the fruit of three thousand years of civilization.[2]

American Zionism in its pre-Brandeis days had reflected the influence of the progressive temper insofar as it identified with political democracy. It was Brandeis, however, who most cogently defined the parallels between Zionism and progressivism. Always the critic of "bigness"—whether manifested in big business, big labor, or big government—because it could stifle individual rights and creativity, Brandeis interpreted the essence of both the American and Zionist dreams to mean equal justice, political democracy, and economic opportunity for the little people. In an age dominated by trusts and monopolies, he urged experimentation through legislation and cooperative economic ventures to prevent basic social values from being swallowed up by the corporate machine. For Brandeis Zionist ideals meant primarily social reform, and he spoke of the efforts of the Palestinian halutzim in the same terms that he used for American reformist ventures. He thought that the Zionists had an advantage in the opportunity to try out new forms of democratic social institutions in a small land.

The compatibility of Zionism with Americanism, that perennial challenge which put Zionists on their defensive, found its justification, according to Brandeis, in the very definition of Americanism. True democracy recognized the value of differentiation and scorned uniformity; if each national or cultural group contributed from its own heritage, American civilization would be best enriched. Thus, from two points of view, insofar as he shared the same ideals and insofar as he kept alive a nationalism which enriched the general culture, the Zionist was a better American than the non-Zionist.

Brandeis's belief in cultural pluralism, elaborated more fully by his associate, Horace Kallen, was not typical of the day. Kallen spoke of the right of different national groups in the United States to perpetuate their cultural heritages, which he likened to orchestral components of a full-bodied American symphony. Most Americans, however, adhered to the melting-pot theory or conformed to the even more popular pattern of Anglo-Saxon domination. Progressives who preached the Herbert Croly message of a single national purpose and frowned upon deviations, or were convinced of the racial superiority of Anglo-Saxons, also differed.

By equating Zionism with Americanism, Brandeis set the American Zionist movement more firmly within its American context. He reinforced that stream of thought, shared by Zionist and non-Zionist alike, which refused to accept for the United States the Herzlian premise of universal anti-Semitism. Zionism was a program that called forth the nobler qualities of its followers; because of it they were better Jews, better Americans, better human beings. But, its moralistic flavor aside, American Zionism remained basically a philanthropic movement. At no time did Brandeis insist that it was incumbent upon American Jews to emigrate to Palestine. As he said, Zionism only gave the Jews the right that any other people enjoyed: to live in the land of their fathers or in some other country.

Brandeis paid little attention to the Jewish traditions and dreams that had given rise to the Zionist ideal. But his leadership brought tremendous gratification to the Zionist rank and file. The penchant of a minority to choose leaders "from the periphery"—that is, from those who enjoyed status in the majority group—was manifested in this instance. And, in 1914, none could match the influence or evoke greater respect in the eyes of non-Jews than the man who had the ear of the president. The Brandeis era marked a dramatic spurt in Zionist growth. The number of shekel payers more than doubled between 1914 and 1915 and reached over thirty thousand; the number of societies affiliated with the FAZ rose from 198 to 270. Besides dazzling the newer immigrants, Brandeis's assumption of office attracted an Americanized group of men and women into the orbit of Zionist leadership. Like him, many participated in reform movements. Julian W. Mack, a federal judge and former professor of law, worked to ameliorate the treatment of juvenile delinquents; Felix Frankfurter, professor of law at Harvard, followed his mentors Holmes and Brandeis in expounding the law as an instrument of social policy; Mrs. Joseph Fels, wife of the affluent soap manufacturer, was a devoted supporter of the single-tax movement and an advocate of land reform. His associates testified to Brandeis's complete absorption in Zionist activities. Under his influence even the administrative routine was reinvigorated, for he sought to operate according to the canons of American efficiency. In 1916, when his appointment to the Supreme Court was confirmed, Brandeis resigned as chairman of the Provisional Executive Committee, but he continued to labor behind the scenes, impressing his point of view on the American Zionist movement for the next five years.

II

In the period óf America's neutrality (1914–17) more than 130 agencies engaged in relief projects for the benefit of European war sufferers. Within the American Jewish community the age-old Jewish tradition of mutual responsibility evoked a response at least equally noteworthy. By the end of 1917 the Joint Distribution Committee (JDC), the clearing house for fund-raising agencies servicing Jewish victims, had amassed some sixteen million dollars.

Zionists, like other Jews, contributed to the relief of European Jewry, but they had a particular concern: to safeguard the new settlements and communal institutions in Palestine. Not only was the economic life of the new settlers crushed when hostilities cut off their foreign markets, but at the beginning of the war Turkish officials gave vent to their blatant anti-Zionism by expulsions and arrests of Jews and destruction of Jewish property. If not for intervention and relief from abroad, Jewish life in Palestine might well have perished.

American Zionists spearheaded drives to raise money and ship food to Palestine, and they influenced the JDC to make generous allocations to Palestine from its combined relief funds. They also set up a Transfer Department, sanctioned by the State Department, which provided, on a nonsectarian basis, the opportunity for Americans to send money directly to Palestine to supply needed services to the disease-ridden land. Zionist leaders on several occasions joined with other prominent American Jews to plead for diplomatic intercession by the State Department on behalf of Palestinian Jewry.

Thanks to Brandeis's influence the Zionists had easy entry to administration circles. The Wilson government was in fact a sympathetic ally, and gave active assistance to the Palestine relief program. The British too were tractable, hoping to swing the sympathies of American Jews to the Allied cause, and permitted food shipments to pass through their blockade. Now in a position of influence, Zionists did not hesitate to apply the same pressures of quiet diplomacy which they found distasteful when employed by the non-Zionist American Jewish stewards.

The problem of Jewish relief indirectly contributed to the cause of political Zionism. The plight of European Jewry appeared particularly serious, since the masses of Eastern Europe lived in areas which lay in the path of the contending armies. They experienced the normal destructive-ness of the military machine and, in addition, anti-Semitic eruptions on the part of both belligerent camps. On humanitarian grounds, Jews and non-Jews in the United States expressed growing sympathy with the need for a Jewish Palestine even as their own country passed bills to restrict the flow of immigrants.

To those who had gone along with Zionism as the practical solution to the persecution of East European Jewry, the Russian Revolution of March 1917 might have appeared a more welcome alternative. But, the American Zionists argued, the collapse of the tsarist regime actually streng-thened the Zionist movement, since Zionist societies were now free to, and did, organize. In an article for the *Maccabaean,* Dr. Chaim Weizmann, the British scientist and prominent Zionist leader, wrote that while a few sup-porters might have been lost, the loss was more than balanced by the fact that those Russians who joined the cause came not out of duress but with the inner strength and conviction of free men.

At the very onset of hostilities Jewish groups began to plan for the peace conference, which, they hoped, would grant full rights to their East European brethren. Zionists quickly latched on to the idea of a democrati-cally elected congress that would send delegates to present the Jewish case. In keeping with the democratic tenets of the Zionist movement, a congress also held out the chance of political advantage. This was the opportunity to organize the hitherto unrepresented East Europeans in the United States and to shape their inchoate ethnic sentiments into a solid nationalist pos-ture. If successful, the Zionists would thereby undercut the power of the anti-Zionist Jewish establishment. Despite formidable opposition from the establishment, an American Jewish Congress was created. Zionist strategy succeeded because American Jews, witnesses to the sacrifices of European Jewish soldiers and civilians, were eager to be counted publicly in support of their coreligionists. The congress episode set an important precedent: the newer and more nationalistic immigrants had used their numerical strength to defeat the affluent entrenched leadership.

III

When the United States entered the war, the crusade for one-hundred-percent Americanism reached a peak. Finding the justification in the need for national unity, Americanization agencies embarked on educational pro-grams aimed at rapid assimilation of the immigrant population and the rooting out of un-American patterns of thought. Congress reflected that antialien mood when, in 1917, it overrode the president's veto of a literacy test for immigrants. In that climate of opinion it would not have been illogical to expect the demise of the Zionist movement, predicated as it was on loyalty to a national group other than the American. Yet American Zionism made rapid strides during the war years.

Part of the explanation of Zionist growth was the fact that the drive for conformity, or monolithic Americanism, was checked by the Wilsonian ideals of self-determination for nationalities and a postwar international democratic forum. Zionists took their cue from those teachings. In 1917 the *Maccabaean* traced the strength of American Zionism to the teachings of American idealism, and American war aims, read through Wilsonian glasses, were equated with the Zionists' own aims:

> Our love and loyalty go out to America not only because it has been a haven of refuge for our oppressed people, but because we have derived inspiration and strength from the ideals and enthusiasms that are America's contribution to modern civilization. The democratic education we have received here has strengthened our own movement for self-emancipation, for we have felt that American ideals gave their sanction to the efforts of any people to secure itself against the future by making such sacrifices today as would render that future worthy.
>
> . . . .
>
> The war implicates the Zionist cause . . . President Wilson has made it clear that we are fighting for the rights of democracies and nationalities . . . Only in a free world will the Zionist cause have an opportunity to be heard and to be dealt with justly.[3]

The Zionists lavished much praise upon the president and exhorted their fellow Jews to show the utmost fealty to the war effort. Enrolled under the Wilsonian banner, they simultaneously supported the nationalist claims of minority groups with greater confidence.

Reasons of diplomacy alone would have dictated a strong pro-Wilson position by the Zionists. Since the beginning of the war Dr. Chaim Weizmann had been negotiating with members of the British cabinet for an official endorsement of Zionist political aims. The British seriously considered the move for a variety of reasons, among which was the desire to win over American and Russian Jewry to the Allied cause. They sought assurances, however, that the Wilson administration would back them. But, since the United States was not at war with Turkey, it could not talk openly of carving up the Turkish Empire. Brandeis, who was pro-Allies from the beginning of the war, was privy to the negotiations, and he, Stephen Wise, and Felix Frankfurter, the Zionists who enjoyed access to Wilson, used their influence to that end. Despite the anti-Zionist posture of Secretary of State Robert Lansing and of his confidential adviser, Colonel Edward M. House, Wilson promised his support to British recognition of a Jewish national home in Palestine. The extent of Wilson's cooperation has been debated, but it is reasonable to assume that the anti-Zionism of the State Department, fed in increasing measure by the influence of Protestant missionaries, would have, if not for the president, quietly quashed the plan. Doubtless the role of serving the providential design of Jewish restoration to Zion appealed to Wilson, the son of a Presbyterian minister. He also appreciated Brandeis's interpretation of a restored Palestine built on the democratic ideals which he, Wilson, was fond of preaching. Aside from offering him a way to thank American Jews for their political support, an endorsement of the Zionist goal gave concrete proof of his concern for national self-determination. And it was justified in terms of wartime diplomacy, for the Allies knew that Germany was scheming to use Palestine in a counterbid for Jewish support.

The product of the British deliberations, the Balfour Declaration, was issued on November 2, 1917 and immediately hailed by Zionists all over the world. American Zionists called it the "Jewish Magna Charta." Transmitted in a letter from British Foreign Minister Arthur Balfour to Lord Lionel Walter Rothschild, the declaration read:

> His Majesty's Government view with favour the establishment in Palestine of a national home for the Jewish people, and will use their best endeavours to facilitate the achievement of this object, it being clearly understood that nothing shall be done which may prejudice the civil and religious rights of existing non-Jewish communities in Palestine, or the rights and political status enjoyed by Jews in any other country.[4]

Replete with ambiguities that would plague Zionist progress for the next thirty years, the Balfour Declaration nevertheless transplanted Herzl's vision from the realm of fantasy to reality.

Public opinion in the United States reacted favorably to the Balfour Declaration, which was regarded by many as the promise of a Jewish state. Of three hundred senators and congressmen who responded to a query by the Zionist Organization of America, most voiced enthusiastic approval. State legislatures were quick to pass resolutions of support. In a statement which inaugurated what would be a consistent pro-Zionist policy, the American Federation of Labor warmly endorsed the idea of a Jewish

homeland. Thomas G. Masaryk, president of the National Czecho-Slovak
Council, expressed his sympathy, and so did Cardinal Gibbons. Even
Theodore Roosevelt, despite his hypernationalism, racist leanings, and
aversion to Wilson, found the whole idea "entirely proper." [5]

But after Wilson's support was made public in 1918 through a letter
to Rabbi Wise, anti-Zionist pressure by Jews, Christians, and Arabs
mounted seriously. Leading Reform rabbis and laymen bitterly attacked
political Zionism as inimical to the liberty and security of American Jewry.
The Central Conference of American Rabbis reaffirmed its traditional opposition to Jewish nationalism; the Reform journal, *American Israelite,*
increased its sniping at the Zionists and their activities. Rabbi David Philip-
son called for a special conference "for the purpose of combatting Zionism," and Congressman Julius Kahn of California submitted a petition to
the president objecting to the grant of territorial sovereignty to the Jews.
Such critics found justification for their fear of Jewish nationalism when
Harvard Professor Albert Bushnell Hart announced that American Jews
would have to "fish or cut bait," [6] choosing between their American citizenship and Zionist loyalties.

Zionists brushed off their opponents with the retort that since the
Balfour Declaration had been endorsed by the president and the majority
in Congress, the argument of dual loyalty had been forever laid to rest.
And, since Zionism had been accepted by the Allies as a war aim, it was
both legitimate and meritorious. On these grounds they could even im-
pugn the patriotism of anti-Zionists!

The Balfour Declaration brought immediate gains to the American
Zionist cause. The number of those who paid their shekel in 1918 reached
a new height of 120,000. The self-styled non-Zionists, speaking through
the influential American Jewish Committee, endorsed the declaration in
moderate but positive terms. New impetus was given to Zionist recruit-
ment efforts for the Jewish Legion, and close to three thousand young men
left to serve with the British army in Palestine. In 1918 the FAZ reorganized itself into the Zionist Organization of America (ZOA), with the individual member rather than the local society as the base unit. Along with
its affiliates the ZOA reported a combined membership within a year of
over 175,000. Simultaneously, it was conducting a vigorous educational
campaign to spread the Zionist message through books and leaflets, lectures
and clubs.

Zionists set their sights on the peace conference, where they hoped to
secure recognition of the Balfour Declaration and the wherewithal to

realize its promise. In preparation, experts studied the resources of Palestine and considered geographic boundaries that would permit the economic absorption of a large Jewish settlement. Under Brandeis's leadership the Americans drafted the principles for guiding the development of the Jewish homeland along the path of social justice. Their program, adopted at the Pittsburgh convention of the ZOA in 1918, demonstrates how the Brandeis administration wove American reformist principles into the Zionist fabric. It read:

1. We declare for political and civil equality irrespective of race, sex, or faith of all the inhabitants of the land.
2. To insure in the Jewish national home in Palestine equality of opportunity we favor a policy which, with due regard to existing rights, shall tend to establish the ownership and control by the whole people of the land, of all natural resources and of all public utilities.
3. All land, owned or controlled by the whole people, should be leased on such conditions as will insure the fullest opportunity for development and continuity of possession.
4. The co-operative principle should be applied so far as possible in the organization of all agricultural, industrial, commercial, and financial undertakings.
5. The fiscal policy shall be framed so as to protect the people from the evils of land speculation and from every other form of financial oppression.
6. The system of free public instruction which is to be established should embrace all grades and departments of education.
7. Hebrew, the national language of the Jewish people, shall be the medium of public instruction.[7]

Although the first six points would have gladdened the heart of any agrarian reformer of the Populist and Progressive eras, the program may have been too American. It was not understood by the immigrant rank and file or by the European Zionists.

American hopes for a speedy and decisive Zionist victory at the Paris peace conference were not realized. Arab spokesmen, citing British promises that conflicted with the Balfour Declaration, presented their counterclaims to the great powers; and the anti-Zionist statements of British and American officials grew louder. The Zionists learned that the Arabs and their friends could turn the principle of national self-determination into an anti-Zionist weapon, for, in fact, the Jews constituted only a small minority in Palestine. True, Wilson remained generally sympathetic, but the larger problems at Paris, his illness, and the mounting resistance to the peace treaty in the United States weakened his ability to offer more positive assistance. Differences also erupted between the European and American Zionists on specific proposals to be submitted to the peacemakers. More militant and idealistic, the Americans talked of mass colonization, generous territorial dimensions, the achievement of self-government status after a transition period under Britain's tutelage, and guidelines like the Pittsburgh Program. Brandeis and other American leaders pressed their case with Allied spokesmen in Paris and London, but the high tide of international idealism, which had contributed to the Balfour Declaration and united Jews in a near-messianic goal, was ebbing. Finally, at the San Remo conference in April 1920, the mandate over Palestine was awarded to Great Britain. The Balfour Declaration was written into the grant, but the terms of the mandate still had to be worked out.

The war years set patterns and raised problems which irrevocably changed the context in which Zionism operated. The most obvious was the emergence of American leadership within the world Zionist movement. Nor was that leadership merely ephemeral. The havoc of war, which impoverished many communities in Europe, pointed up the need for the affluent American community to assume greater responsibilities. Equally important was the beginning of official American involvement with political Zionism. Although the Balfour Declaration and the San Remo decision dealt with an area in which Great Britain had been the paramount Western power, United States opinion was weighed in connection with both pronouncements. Significant also was the fact that Zionism received the support of the president and Congress but not of the State Department. Finally, as the episode of the American Jewish Congress proved, the Jewish immigrant masses were demanding greater control over communal affairs. If they challenged the American-born leaders of the Brandeis era, the distinctively American flavor imparted to Zionist ideology could well evaporate. Therefore, the course of Zionism during the next decade would be linked both to developments of American foreign policy and to the internal evolution of the American Jewish community.

3

Postwar Decline

During the 1920s Zionists faced a crucial test: could they take advantage of the international recognition they had won and the promises they had secured? In the face of Arab counterclaims and British counterpromises, could they carry out a program that would establish in fact a Jewish homeland in Palestine? The question could be asked specifically of American Zionists, for in the postwar era their numbers, economic influence, and political security made them the focal point of any concerted Jewish endeavor.

I

The Brandeis-led ZOA met the challenge head on. Brandeis sounded the theme: "The work of the great Herzl was completed at San Remo. . . . The rest lies with us. The task before us . . . is the task of reconstruction." [1] Political and educational work could now be ended, he insisted, and the energies of the Zionist movement concentrated on the manifold tasks of rehabilitating the land. Spurred on by his findings during a visit to Palestine in 1919, he outlined blueprints for projects like afforestation, eradication of malaria, inquiries into industrial and commercial development. In true progressive fashion his program underscored efficiency, scientific management, and expertise. In effect it would have meant a drastic revision of Zionist thinking and activity.

At the 1920 World Zionist Conference in London, the position of the Americans isolated them from the Europeans. Disagreements flared up on many issues—cultural programs, fund-raising, organizational structure, office-holding. The Europeans, more committed to the socialist ideal of *kibbutziut,* opposed the Americans' insistence on attracting private capital

25

investment. They also resented Brandeis's inflexibility and his refusal to assume an active role in the leadership of the world movement.

Ideologically the rift went deeper. The Americans rejected the European-held philosophy of diaspora nationalism, or the idea that the Jews constituted a political group in countries outside Palestine, and the view that the World Zionist Organization functioned in a political sense to unite world Jewry. Denying the applicability of those theories to American Jews, they revealed how strongly the American environment had influenced their thinking. To the Europeans it appeared that the Americans were reading themselves out of the mainstream of Jewish development; some muttered about an American Zionist Monroe Doctrine. Dr. Weizmann, leader of the Europeans, summed up the seriousness of the rift by saying: "There is no bridge between Washington and Pinsk." [2]

The Brandeis administration continued to push its own approach in the United States, abolishing its education department, cutting down its publications, and giving little support to its affiliated organizations. A trade and industry department was created to supply information on business opportunities in Palestine, and the *New Palestine* (organ of the ZOA) abounded in news about investment experiments and labor needs in that country. Plans were also made to set up investment corporations in Jewish centers throughout the United States. Since these projects directly challenged the fund-raising procedure adopted by the World Zionist Organization, a conflict developed within American ranks between the pro-Brandeis and pro–World Zionist Organization factions. The latter group, long resentful of what they considered high-handedness and undemocratic procedure by the leadership, justified their stand in terms of world Jewish solidarity. They were strengthened considerably with the arrival of a Zionist delegation to the United States in April 1921. Dr. Weizmann headed the delegation; Dr. Albert Einstein's presence contributed to its prestige. The Zionist leaders were widely acclaimed as they toured the United States. New York honored Dr. Weizmann by presenting him with the keys to the city; Weizmann Days were celebrated in numerous Jewish communities. Officially Weizmann's purpose was to launch Keren Hayesod (the Palestine Restoration Fund) in the United States and to awaken public interest in the Hebrew University, but his trip served to mobilize the opposition to Brandeis and his policies. Two months later, at the ZOA convention in Cleveland, the delegates refused to vote their confidence in the administration. Brandeis and his lieutenants submitted their resignations, closing a chapter in American Zionist history.

The change in leadership was more than the result of differences in program. In broader perspective it was a reflection of the growing pains of the American Jewish community. That community in 1920 numbered close to three and a half million, with the preponderant majority of East European origin. The Zionists among them had fashioned their ideology from a two-thousand-year-old cultural heritage. Proud of Brandeis, they nevertheless did not come to Zionism by way of American reform, nor did most of them grasp the meaning of his progressive principles. They could not divorce themselves from European Zionist thinking, and if the issue were joined between Washington and Pinsk, they would vote for Pinsk. On the other hand, the war had speeded up their integration into American society and had temporarily cut off the flow of immigrants, which hitherto had served to keep the entire group closer for a longer period to Old World ways. More acclimatized now to the United States, they were ready to assert their independence of the older American stratum.

One move along the road to independence was the creation of a permanent American Jewish Congress in 1922. Although the original congress had been scheduled to adjourn upon completing its mission to the peace conference, a sufficiently large number of delegates voted to keep the group in existence for the purpose of defending the rights of Jews all over the world. As such the agency directly challenged the leadership of the self-appointed stewards of German background. According to the congress's foremost leader, Stephen Wise, it was too late to return to "the undemocratic, un-American, un-Jewish method of dictation from above." [3]

The price of independence was high. The rift within the organization was a blow to morale. Membership fell off drastically, in part because the older American element would not follow foreign-born leaders. More important, the Zionists lost personalities tried in the ways of interceding privately with the government.

II

Zionists could have used "friends in court" to help offset the antipathy of the State Department to their cause. When Harding's normalcy replaced Wilson's internationalism, America shunned the responsibilities of world power and spurned moralistic commitments. Humanitarian diplomacy, the tool used on countless occasions by American Jews when appealing for government aid on behalf of Jews abroad, was quietly shelved. With respect to Zionism the State Department also retreated, and the views of Secretary Lansing, whom Wilson originally bypassed in the negotiations leading to the Balfour Declaration, emerged victorious. Oil interests with their eyes on concessions in Palestine, necessarily impinging on Zionist designs, reinforced the department's desire to preserve the open door in the mandated area but to steer clear of politics. Simultaneously, in Professor Selig Adler's words, "Consular reports from the Near East frequently reported communism among the Jewish pioneers, drew invidious distinctions between 'Jews' and 'Zionists,' showed increasing pro-Arab sympathy, questioned the economic absorptive capacity of the land, and constantly expressed fear for the safety of the Christian shrines. British pronouncements paring down the Balfour Declaration were secretly applauded." [4]

True, in 1922 a joint congressional resolution, sponsored by Senator Henry Cabot Lodge and Representative Hamilton Fish, Jr., gave formal American approval to "the establishment in Palestine of a national home for the Jewish people." Zionists who had campaigned for the resolution with the help of Christian sympathizers were elated, since Congress was not deterred by the State Department or the adverse testimony of Arab supporters and anti-Zionist Jews. The Zionists hoped that the move would facilitate adoption of the mandate terms by the world powers. Britain liked the resolution, too, since it fell in with its design to tie the United States politically to a Near Eastern settlement. But whatever motives prompted them, congressmen insisted the resolution meant no commitment or foreign entanglement. And it did not alter State Department policy. When asked by a foreign diplomat whether the resolution represented the views of the United States government on the mandate, a State Department official merely smiled.

Nor did the Anglo-American treaty of 1924, which included the preamble of the mandate and thus explicitly sanctioned the Balfour Declaration, hold out any assurances of American assistance. It sought merely to place the rights of American citizens in Palestine on an equal footing with those enjoyed by citizens of countries that were League of Nations members, and it specified that the terms of the mandate could not be altered without United States consent. That provision was interpreted to mean general American interests only.

On the surface it appeared that by these acts America had affirmed a moral commitment to Zionism, but it is equally plausible that it had only acquiesced in the new British interpretation of the Balfour Declaration. A Jewish state—which was how most people read the declaration in 1917—gave way after the Churchill White Paper of 1922 to some vague home, or colony, or territorial enclave within Palestine. In its postwar isolationist mood the United States tried to have its cake and eat it too; it insisted on the rights of a world power and the privileges of League membership without the corresponding responsibilities or involvement.

In the interests of both the Jewish minorities in Europe and the Zionist cause, it would have been logical for American Jewry to strive to keep the United States an active guardian of world order. Jewish groups, however, organized no popular support for the League of Nations or American adherence thereto. Jews as a body were not yet identified with the Democratic party, which in 1920 bore the mantle of Wilson's internationalism. Like other Americans they too wrapped themselves in an isolationist cocoon.

For the East European Jews who had immigrated after 1880, consolidation of social and economic position was an overriding concern. They moved out of their original ghetto neighborhoods, fashioned elaborate systems of philanthropic agencies, and went on a spree of synagogue building. Seeds of Zionist strength were scattered in the layers of community growth—the Jewish Institute of Religion, a Reform seminary of Zionist sympathy; the increase in Conservative synagogues manned by rabbis trained in the Schechterian tradition; the American Jewish Congress, virtually identical in leadership with the ZOA, which fused Zionism with broader defense activities. In addition, control over communal agencies was shifting, as the East Europeans, more sympathetic to Zionism, gradually replaced the older German element. These trends, however, had yet to ripen.

III

The mood of American society in the postwar era raised problems for Jews of more immediate concern than a Jewish Palestine. The recoil from idealism in the aftermath of the war, and the economic and social dislocations of the Wilson years which society still had to absorb, reworked the wartime one-hundred-percent Americanism into an extreme antiforeign posture. Concepts of pluralism were eclipsed by insistence on monolithic conformity. Nativism and racism flourished in what has been fittingly called the "Anglo-Saxon decade."

Even before the Red Scare of 1919–20 reached its height, Jews were singled out as objects of suspicion on charges linking them with bolshevism. A Senate subcommittee heard testimony that specifically referred to the Jews of New York's Lower East Side as the "predominant element" of the Bolshevik movement in the United States. The Jew-Bolshevik nexus was repeated in magazines and by private groups and set the stage for the popular reception of the *Protocols of the Elders of Zion.* The *Protocols,* a tract which purportedly revealed how an international Jewish conspiracy schemed for world domination, had been concocted by tsarist agents in prewar Russia. The book made its way to the United States, where it was republished and picked up by superpatriotic groups. Although it was shortly exposed as fraudulent, it was kept alive by Henry Ford, who used it until 1927 as the basis for an anti-Semitic campaign in his newspaper, the *Dearborn Independent.* In a decade when rural forces fought the growing control by urban America, Ford found a ready audience. Using terms like *foreign, atheist, communist,* and *manipulating financier* to depict the Jews, his diatribes provided an outlet for the resentment and frustration of fundamentalist agrarian society.

American Jews were severely jolted by the wave of anti-Semitism, which they had previously associated almost exclusively with Central and Eastern Europe. Nor was anti-Semitism limited to smear attacks by Ford or the Ku Klux Klan. It was manifest in laws that established immigration quotas on racial lines, the exclusion of Jews from the consular service, the numerus clausus for Jews in universities and professional schools, and the rigid barriers against Jews in the managerial economy. Even echoes of the medieval ritual-murder charge were heard in 1928 in connection with the disappearance of a small child in Massena, New York.

The Jewish response to anti-Semitism took different forms. There were those who refused to dignify the charges by offering any defense, and, at the opposite pole, those who were impelled to negate their Jewishness. Most agreed that Jewish behavior had not triggered the situation, but some blamed Jewish nationalists for arousing prejudice. Dr. Cyrus Adler, a tireless worker for Jewish causes, bitterly cited the parades, flags, and congresses which called unwanted attention to Jews at large. Those who formulated a defense did not always agree on tactics, debating whether quiet pressure or flamboyant publicity would be a better means of presenting their case. For the most part, however, a rationalist approach was followed in meeting the attacks. Jewish leaders refuted the anti-Semitic charges and showed how they deviated from American tradition. By making the issue an American one, they called upon Christians of goodwill to voice protests.

Although anti-Semitism forced Jews to wrestle with the problem of Jewish identity, it did not shake the belief, shared by Zionists and non-Zionists, that America was not exile, that America was exempt from the postulates negating survival in the diaspora. Anti-Semitism never became a Zionist tool to argue against a future for Jews in the United States or to prod for emigration to Palestine. In 1921 Rabbi Abba Hillel Silver commented on the anti-Semitic outbursts at a Zionist meeting, but he went only so far: "We are going to respond to every attack upon our people, to every libel and every slander, by more Jewishness, by more schools and synagogues and by more intensive and loyal work in Palestine." [5] A year later Zionist spokesmen, testifying on behalf of the Lodge-Fish resolution, specifically asserted that American Jews had no desire to leave the United States for Palestine.

No doubt the "more Jewish" posture advocated by Rabbi Silver and identification with the Zionist ideal offered emotional support in face of discrimination. The profounder implications of that approach were articulated best in the 1920s by two men of letters, Ludwig Lewisohn and Maurice Samuel. Lewisohn's fiction and Samuel's essays [6] dealt with themes that, in the authors' minds, in no way excluded twentieth-century America: the inability of the Jew to escape his Jewish heritage, the inadequacy of assimilation for insuring equality, the stunting effect of assimilation on the Jewish personality, the chasm between Jewish and gentile values. Both affirmed that Zionism was more than a means for bringing Jewish ideals to fruition. It also served to make the emancipated Jew a whole and self-respecting individual by integrating him with his past. Lewisohn and Samuel were the exceptions, and the thrust of their message—the personal need of American Jews for Zionism—did not significantly influence the course of the American Zionist movement of those years.

IV

The pressure of anti-Semitism reinforced the tendency of the American Jewish community to concentrate on strengthening its own position within American society. Wary of political agitation that might give credence to the image of the "international Jew," many Jews purposely steered clear of the Zionist movement. To offset the ensuing sharp decline in membership Zionists had to alter the tone of their ideology in order to attract support. The cause they propagated in the 1920s was a response more to the immediate desires of American Jews than the needs of the Zionist program.

Officially, repudiation of Brandeis's leadership meant American Zionist acquiescence in the aims and methods of the World Zionist Organization. Under the new administration, headed by Louis Lipsky, Abraham

Goldberg, Meyer Weisgal, and Morris Rothenberg, the ZOA formally resumed a broad program encompassing educational activities and propaganda work. In fact, however, the ZOA functioned primarily as a fund-raising agency. Political Zionism—that is, propaganda campaigns for independent Jewish statehood—was suspended; the theory of diaspora nationalism, with its implications of international political unity, was ignored. Zionist work became almost exclusively Palestine-centered, with energies concentrated on financial support of material and scientific enterprises in that country. Since fund-raising superseded the development of national consciousness, businessmen replaced intellectuals in directing the organization. Brandeis was defeated in 1921, and although his faction did not return to the movement until the end of the decade, his practical and apolitical approach won out.

In revamping its program the ZOA offered an agreeable compromise. It served American Jews who desired a means of identifying as Jews without the embarrassing implications of ethnic distinctiveness. By making Zionism purely a philanthropic venture it gave them a cause which could be respected and approved by Christians as well as Jews. Philanthropy, after all, was a stock American middle-class virtue, and there was nothing un-American about raising money for a Hebrew University, or for hospitals, or even to float Tel Aviv municipal bonds. In the Brandeis era Zionism was equated with Americanism because of the democratic posture of the movement. In the 1920s Zionism was American because it was businesslike, acultural in emphasis, and philanthropic. By tailoring its approach to fit the temper of the decade, the ZOA was able to insure its own continuity.

The narrower function of fund-raising gave rise to its own set of problems. True, when stripped of political and propagandistic trappings, raising money for Palestine was facilitated. Between 1921 and 1929 Keren Hayesod amassed over ten million dollars, or fifty-five percent of its funds, in the United States. But one could give money to Palestine without joining a Zionist organization, and bereft of any other serious cause Zionists could not regain the high wartime membership. In 1925 the ZOA reported a membership of twenty-seven thousand; the figure soon began to drop, and by 1929, before the impact of the Crash was felt, it sank to eighteen thousand. In addition, Zionists had to compete with other groups for contributions, and they never raised more than a fraction of what the JDC collected during the same period. Even fund-raising, to be successful, presupposed an ideology that was understood by the community. For example, when the JDC launched a special campaign in 1926 for the purpose of settling Russian Jews in the Crimea, the Zionists were hard put to show that support of Palestine was more worthwhile than investments for the future of Jewry in the diaspora. Without an educational program, the American community would not grasp the differences between palliative relief and long-range constructive reform. A cultural program was also essential if, as many of the movement's intellectuals had postulated, Zionism were to contribute to the vitalization of Judaism in the United States. One Zionist commented sadly at the end of the decade that the new methods had resulted in a watered-down, contentless American Judaism. Furthermore, since American Jewry was not stimulated to think of Zionism as a means of achieving self-fulfillment, only a handful attempted the life of halutzim in Palestine.[7] Dr. Weizmann later admitted the harm done to American Zionism: "We have abused America as a moneygiving machine. Under the pressure to which America has been subject, it has not developed an adequate, healthy, vigorous Zionism."[8]

Although the ZOA still constituted the most powerful Zionist group in the United States, its activities were no longer synonymous with the scope of American Zionism. Unity of action, which had been sustained among the different Zionist factions by the political issues and glamorous leadership of the war years, would reappear only in time of crisis. Other movements were at work, spurred on by developments within the Palestinian Jewish community and by changes within the ZOA itself. The Brandeis faction, for example, pushed its economic schemes through independent organizations like the Palestine Development Council and the Palestine Economic Corporation. Thousands of others invested in the American Zion Commonwealth, which, during the 1920s, became the largest buyer of land for Jewish settlement in Palestine. Youth, largely neglected by the ZOA, formed its own groups, some with a *halutziut* bent. Even Hadassah became increasingly autonomous, running its separate educational, philanthropic, and propaganda programs. The religious and labor Zionists stepped up their own programs, organizing women's affiliates and, unlike the ZOA, undertaking new educational projects. Labor Zionism leaped forward during the twenties by setting up a separate nexus between American Jewish labor and Palestinian workers. And unique ventures like the establishment of the Hebrew University spawned their own committees of friends and benefactors.

V

The fund-raising character of American Zionism helped blur the distinction between Zionist and non-Zionist. As nationalist talk decreased and the ideal of a state dimmed—a situation reinforced by the British White

Paper of 1922 and the insignificant influx of Jews into Palestine—sympathy with Zionism (= Palestinianism) spread more extensively throughout the American Jewish community. Reform Jews who were non-Zionist, like the prominent personalities of the American Jewish Committee, had no qualms about contributing to cultural and scientific undertakings in Palestine. And, since the terms of the mandate legalized Jewish immigration and landholding in Palestine, they, like all who were interested in preserving international order, could help protect those rights. They were ready to listen, therefore, when Dr. Weizmann proposed a formal partnership between Zionists and non-Zionists for the upbuilding of Palestine. Weizmann, who hoped for greater support from America, sought to involve the affluent stratum of American Jewry in the formulation and administration of policy and thereby open up untapped financial resources.

In 1923 Weizmann began negotiations with the two leading non-Zionists, Louis Marshall, president of the American Jewish Committee and nationally recognized Jewish spokesman, and Felix Warburg, banker and philanthropist. Weizmann's plan was to bring non-Zionists into the Jewish Agency, a body authorized by the mandate terms, and originally identical with the World Zionist executive, to advise the British authorities in Palestine. After six years of intermittent conferences and talks, an enlarged Jewish Agency was created. Non-Zionists were granted fifty percent of the seats on its council and executive; forty percent of the non-Zionists were to be Americans.

The enlarged Jewish Agency did not fulfill the expectations of its founders. Zionist domination continued despite the parity principle, and the non-Zionists bitterly resented mere paper equality. On the other side were those Zionists who criticized the compromise in ideology which the partnership with antistatists signified. Stephen Wise also bemoaned that the new body killed Zionism as a democratic movement by handing it over to a "millionaire-trusteeship." [9] And when fund-raising was taken over by the agency, American Zionism stood to lose its only significant function.

Marshall died only weeks after the agreement for an enlarged Jewish Agency was concluded, and Weizmann shortly retired from the Zionist executive. With the two ablest statemen gone, the Jewish Agency could not rise above internal friction. At the same time, hopes for substantial financial contributions from the United States waned with the crash of 1929 and onset of the depression.

The Arab riots in Palestine in 1929 and their aftermath illustrated the various developments relating to Zionism which had taken shape since the war. Both the Arabs and the British were emboldened by the failure of the Zionists to create a substantial settlement. The former were not afraid to attack; the latter were ready to whittle down still further the Jewish rights agreed to under the mandate. The newly enlarged Jewish Agency was scarcely a deterrent. Moderate and judicious in presenting the Jewish case to the British, it aroused criticism and division of opinion within Jewish ranks. The American Zionists in particular appeared far less formidable than they had in 1917. They staged rallies, inveighed in speeches and the press against British policies, passed resolutions, cooperated with non-Zionists in collecting relief funds, and sought help from Washington. The State Department, however, was unmoved. Despite the fact that about a dozen Americans had been killed in the riots, President Hoover's administration saw no reason to pressure England to prevent further violence. A suggestion for sending an American cruiser to the Near East—supported by several congressmen and by Ambassador Dawes in London—was turned down. Nor would Secretary of State Henry Stimson agree with the Zionists that the provisions of the Anglo-American treaty of 1924 gave the United States the right to protest the new interpretation by the British of their responsibilities as mandatory power. Refusal to become involved meant, in practical terms, sanction of British policy in Palestine. The isolationist mood of the country was reinforced by the economic crisis, and there was no chance of arousing the public, Jews as well as non-Jews, in order to override the State Department. Rabbi Stephen Wise summed up the position of American Zionism in 1930 in pessimistic terms:

> There is a complete lull in things Zionistic in America. . . . The Zionist Organization is gone. . . . My pessimism is not of the moment. The British government's conduct for ten years by its Palestine administration, the incapacity or unwillingness of the Zionist leadership to deal vigorously with the problem, the Arab riots . . . plus the killing of Zionism as a democratic mass movement . . . have robbed me of my faith. It [the Zionist hope] will come to pass, I have no doubt, but only despite us of the Diaspora who have miserably trifled with a great situation.[10]

4

Years of Crisis

I

The onset of the Great Depression in the early 1930s had a discernible impact on American Jewish attitudes toward Zionism and Palestine. Economic hardships besetting individual families eclipsed all other concerns. The unemployment rate of Jews rose sharply, their welfare agencies were taxed with mounting burdens. Zionism faded to peripheral interest, and the payment of even token dues to a Zionist organization—in days when education and hospital care became luxuries—was drastically curtailed. On the other hand, for material reasons alone Palestine appealed to some Jews as it had never before. Despite the worldwide depression, the economy of that country was flourishing, and between 1933 and 1935 over three thousand Jews from America made their way there in the hope of improving their economic lot.

The challenge facing Americans was not merely to work out of another of the periodic depressions that economists regarded as a more or less unavoidable consequence of the inexorable workings of the business cycle. Given the seriousness of the crisis, many asked whether capitalism had finally proved its bankruptcy. Did the failure of capitalism also doom the future of political democracy? Did America's only hope for recovery lie in an "ism" from the left or right, along the lines of Russian communism or Italian fascism? Americans looked for panaceas in a variety of causes and, during the decade, flirted with novel schemes of both native and foreign origin. Huey Long's Share-the-Wealth, Upton Sinclair's EPIC ("End Poverty in California") movement, and Dr. Francis Townsend's Old Age Revolving Pensions were but three of the better known formulas.

Activist Jews read the issue in terms of social justice, the characteristic guise of Jewish messianism in the modern world, and some found an outlet in socialist and communist organizations. For those, like the Jewish writers of proletarian novels (e.g., Michael Gold, the author of *Jews without Money*), the Jewish question was swallowed up in the universal problem of the "increasing misery of the masses."

Most American Jews, however, gave their loyalty to the New Deal. Workers and shopkeepers, they shared a middle-class outlook which rejected radical leftist dogma. They looked rather to Roosevelt, the American patrician who spoke to the common man, and they shared his desire to patch up democratic capitalism and extend its benefits. They interpreted the New Deal as a social cause that transcended politics and, as Professor William Leuchtenburg summed up, offered a place in the sun to others besides the WASP property-holder. The success of the New Deal, they believed, would assure them the opportunity of living comfortably both as Americans and as Jews.

Roosevelt consciously built up his following among minority groups as he forged the urban backbone of the Democratic party. His chief advisers included Henry Morgenthau, Jr., Felix Frankfurter, and Samuel Rosenman; his administration put no numerus clausus on talent or ideas. The journalist Judd Teller has described the Jews who flocked to Roosevelt's agencies:

> Some of these Jews came from Harvard, Princeton, and Yale where their percentage had been kept deliberately low, and were generally of the German-Jewish upper middle-class. But they shared the social passion of another kind of Jew who was also appointed to these Washington posts, that of the lower middle-class and the proletariat, . . . graduates of the University of Chicago . . . and from New York's City College. . . . For many of the young Jews this was their first encounter with Americans of other faiths in a close day-to-day working relationship. This was also the first encounter of the others with Jews.[1]

Given the exciting goal of reconstructing American society and the chance to participate in that reconstruction, Jews of ability chose government service above involvement in Jewish affairs. The result, according to Teller, left the mediocrities in control of the Jewish, including Zionist, agencies, and their programs correspondingly became more insignificant and unappealing.

The ineptitude of Zionist leadership notwithstanding, a segment of Jewish youth found their place in the various youth groups of that movement. Unlike the first such groups, which sprang up before 1920, those of the 1930s—affiliates of the general, labor, and religious Zionist organizations—catered to a membership predominantly of American-born and English-speaking students. They provided teenagers and young adults with a wide variety of cultural and social activities, which stressed Jewish identity and national self-consciousness. Like more general American youth movements, they subscribed to antiwar and antitotalitarian beliefs. The labor and religious groups went further and taught the ideal of *halutziut,* or pioneering. Hashomer Hatzair, the only one without a parent organization, even demanded a firm commitment to settle in Palestine as a condition of membership.

The appeal of *halutziut* made sense in the thirties. To a generation approaching adulthood during the days of Hitler and the depression, it offered an ideology of hope, of advancing beyond systems which had gone bankrupt. *Halutziut,* incidentally, did not necessarily mean Palestine. In 1933 Golda Meyerson, who became Israel's prime minister some thirty-five years later, defined *halutziut* to a convention of Young Poale Zion Alliance as social pioneering anywhere in the world. Most, however, interpreted it as pioneering in Palestine, in the form of manual labor and some sort of cooperative settlement. As such it fired the idealism and incipient rebelliousness of middle-class youth by stressing the dignity of labor above professional or white-collar careers, the value of "doing" above academic training. *Halutziut* reinterpreted the Jewish framework of its partisans, substituting Hebrew for Yiddish and the promise of a nation reborn for the nostalgia of the ghetto.

Those who chose *halutziut* prepared seriously in the United States for a life of pioneering. They attended experimental summer camps and trained intensively on cooperative farms set up for that very purpose. From Palestine came special emissaries to guide them in their preparation. Perhaps the most famous was Enzo Sereni, who later served as a special agent of the British army during World War II. He was captured and executed by the Nazis after parachuting behind enemy lines in Hungary.

The dedication of the prospective pioneers drew sympathy and support from public figures. Secretary of the Interior Harold Ickes said that the pioneers, like the American people, were fighting for a "new deal." [2] Justice Brandeis contributed five thousand dollars to Hashomer Hatzair for the purchase of land in Palestine for settlement, and in 1937 the Americans founded a new kibbutz and named it Ein ha-Shofet ("Fount of the Justice") in his honor.

Of some six thousand Americans who immigrated to Palestine between 1932 and 1945, halutzim constituted only a small portion. But their story added a new dimension to American Zionism.

It was no coincidence that Reconstructionism, a philosophy of Judaism expounded by Professor Mordecai M. Kaplan, proved so popular with young Jewish intellectuals during the thirties. Just as the New Deal applied pragmatism to politics, so Reconstructionism drew upon the teachings of John Dewey to formulate a faith palatable to the native-born, educated, secularized American Jew. Kaplan, who influenced a generation of rabbis, teachers, and social workers through his teaching posts at the Jewish Theological Seminary and the Graduate School of Jewish Social Work, and his work with the Bureau of Jewish Education, translated much of Jewish theology into humanistic terms. He stressed the creative powers of the individual, the functional role of tradition and religious law, and the struggle for social betterment as the path to salvation. Like Dewey's, his philosophy was man-centered and progress-oriented.

Reconstructionism also subscribed to cultural Zionism. Kaplan defined Judaism as a civilization which drew its spiritual strength from Palestine, the historical homeland and the future home. Zionism was a movement to bring about the renascence of Jewish culture and ideals, radiating from the hub, Palestine, throughout the diaspora. Building upon the doctrine of cultural pluralism, Kaplan saw no reason why the Jews, a people rather than members of a religious denomination, could not live in accordance with their ethnic heritage in the United States. But they were Americans first in all their loyalties.

For our discussion, Kaplan's views are significant because they encompassed what one sociologist aptly described as the folk religion of American Jews. Kaplan enunciated what most Jews subscribed to, hitherto in vague, emotional, and undefined form. With respect to Zionism, American Jews were more certain since the 1920s of what it did not mean—dual political loyalties, a commitment to settle in Palestine, despair over a future in America—than what it meant. They needed Zionism to fill psychological needs; it served as a focus for identification, a link with the Jewish heritage, and an insulation against gentile rejection. Reconstructionism recognized that even the native-born children of the East European immigrants could not easily discard their ethnic ties, and it provided a modern rationale for those sentiments.

The "latent" Zionism articulated by Reconstructionism pervaded wide American Jewish circles. Yiddish, Hebrew, and Anglo-Jewish periodicals were increasingly pro-Zionist. Parents sent their children to Hebrew schools —Hebrew, the language of the nationalist revival—where the teachers were usually Zionists. Pupils sang songs and put on plays about Herzl and the pioneers and contributed their pennies to Zionist causes. Slowly modern Hebrew made its way into the public high schools and colleges. In specific instances latent Zionism was reinforced by organizational projects. The Hebrew Youth Cultural Federation organized a serious dramatic group, which patterned itself upon Habimah, the Palestinian troupe. At the Century of Progress Exhibition of 1934 and at the New York World's Fair of 1939, the Zionist themes of the Jewish exhibits were brought home to thousands of Jewish and non-Jewish spectators. The rebuilding of Palestine was also the subject of a film, *Land of Promise,* which ran for many weeks in 1935 at a New York theater. Though none could deny the concomitant impact of nazism in evoking Jewish nationalist sentiments, latent Zionism was the bedrock upon which Zionist organizations would be able to build their impressive forces during the war years.

II

Overshadowing the depression in its implications for American Jews was the entrenchment of nazism in Germany. Hitler assumed control of that country in 1933 with a program based on an irrational appeal to race and blood purity. The non-Aryan, specifically the Jew, was the Nazi target. What had begun as acts of vandalism committed by Hitler's followers against Jews in the 1920s developed into local ordinances proscribing Jewish practices. Once in control of the federal government the Nazis proceeded to drive Jews out of the professions and from public office. In 1935 the Nuremberg Laws directly translated the racist teachings into public law by forbidding contact between Jew and non-Jew. German Jews were defenseless in the face of such measures. Their affluence notwithstanding, they could neither destroy nazism nor escape its persecution. Since racism was made the base of anti-Semitism, even conversion to Christianity was futile.

The onset of Nazi anti-Semitism jolted the American Jewish community. No longer could the Nazi movement be discounted as the work of a few hoodlums or, as Louis Marshall had described it in the 1920s, as a German Ku Klux Klan. Germany was not backward tsarist Russia, where sporadic pogroms had been commonplace after 1880. And German Jews were, since the nineteenth century, the most highly cultured and assimilated Jewish group in the world.

The problem was compounded by the reverberations of Nazi anti-Semitic propaganda in the United States. Directed and sustained by the German embassy and consulates, the message of hate was preached through Nazi-type organizations, like the German-American Bund, and German and English publications. The Nazi machine reached beyond the German Americans. It sought out and cultivated American sympathizers and even helped to defray their expenses. Congressman Louis T. McFadden was spurred on to deliver a vicious anti-Semitic speech in Congress a few days after he met with a Nazi agent. The Reverend Gerald B. Winrod, leader of the Defenders of the Christian Faith, was invited to visit Germany, where he was lavishly entertained. Operating an international propaganda network from Erfurt, Germany, the Nazis also set up "shirt" organizations, parallel to the Brown Shirts of Hitler's cadres, in different countries. The United States had its Silver Shirts under a self-styled fuehrer, William Dudley Pelley.

Encouraged by the Nazis and with the opportunity to capitalize on the fears and frustrations spawned by the depression, anti-Semitic groups multiplied rapidly. The American Jewish Committee counted over five hundred such groups in 1939. Except for Father Charles Coughlin's followers, their members were mostly old-stock Protestant, urban, and middle class. Coughlin, the Canadian-born priest known to millions from his weekly radio broadcast and his newspaper, *Social Justice,* used those media to spread hatred of the Jew among the lower-class, urban, Catholic elements. A former supporter of Roosevelt and the New Deal, he openly subscribed to fascist teachings after 1938. Drawing his material from the fabrications of the *Protocols* and the Nazi propaganda machine, Coughlin pushed his attacks into the city streets. Vendors of *Social Justice* purposely incited brawls with their anti-Semitic taunts. They and their sympathizers, organized in the Christian Front, held anti-Semitic street meetings and staged anti-Jewish boycotts.

In addition to the openly anti-Semitic organizations there were also those which subsumed their Jew-hatred under a patriotic guise, thereby appealing to a more respectable element. But all groups circulated the stock anti-Semitic charges, and the *Protocols of the Elders of Zion* enjoyed a new burst of popularity. Public-opinion polls revealed that the image of the Jew bore traces of the smear attacks: the Jew was accused of economic greed and deceit, pushiness, clannishness, and vulgarity; he was labeled both Communist and warmonger. German Jewish helplessness in the face of Hitler had weakened the Jewish position outside Germany too. The non-Jew might pity innocent victims, but evidence of vulnerability often bred contempt.

Against that background Zionist ideology stood to gain. Germany had fallen victim to anti-Semitism, and the American Jew under attack was less confident of his place in society. Had those who preached the futility of life in the diaspora been proved correct? Ludwig Lewisohn thought so. In an article appearing in the *Nation* in 1933 he bitterly described how German Jewry had by assimilation sold out spiritually to their persecutors. He pointed his warnings at American Jews: Jewish attempts to obliterate the differences between themselves and non-Jews resulted only in making the aggressor stronger and the persecuted more defenseless.

Some Jews, who were witnessing anti-Semitism for the first time, found an answer in Zionism. Identification with an activist Jewish movement provided the comfort of group solidarity in the face of discrimination and the wherewithal to assert one's Jewishness with pride. A young reader of the *New Palestine,* describing himself as an "average American Jew," expressed his need of Zionism in the following way:

> Many . . . young Jews, as myself, have been startlingly awakened to the threat to our existence by the horribly persistent forward march of Hitlerism abroad and by the rise of American Hitlerism through the medium of Coughlinism and Bundism . . . We are not intellectuals conscious of a dream of Jewish national life, but neither are we playboys. We should like to be some sort of American Zionists enjoying Zionism in an American way.[3]

The key words were "in an American way." American Jews, including Zionists, were more frightened than angered by the rise in anti-Semitism. Since they refused to give up their faith in America, they grew more cautious and apologetic, concerned above all with how other Americans regarded them. A liberal Christian like Professor Alvin Johnson reinforced that trend when he advised his Jewish friends to play down Zionism and other forms of Jewish separatism.

Unlike Lewisohn, most Jews would not admit to the bankruptcy of diaspora living even in Germany. To announce, at least before 1938, that German Jews had to pack up and leave Germany en masse was in effect agreeing with Hitler that Jews had no future there. It could also strengthen anti-Semitic currents elsewhere by showing that the Jews never really felt rooted in countries outside Palestine.

Accordingly, the ideology of American Zionism did not change during the thirties. Zionist leaders always insisted that their movement was more than a response to emergencies involving foreign Jews, but their program remained basically philanthropic. They concentrated on building up Palestine as a haven for the persecuted, and American Jews responded generously as the crisis intensified. (The membership of the ZOA alone rose from eighty-nine hundred in 1933 to forty-three thousand in 1939.) Insofar as they were able, Zionists also chose to fight nazism and American anti-Semitism. And the very act of fighting affirmed that a Jewish state was not the only alternative left to the Jews.

III

Zionism drew consistent and impressive support from modern Orthodox and Conservative congregations. Religious services and schools, sermons and pronouncements by rabbinical organizations—all reflected the pervasive influence of the Zionist ideal. Orthodox Jews affiliated with the ZOA as well as Mizrachi, attesting to a loyalty transcending pure denominationalism. In 1938 the ZOA acknowledged its close ties with the Rabbinical Assembly (Conservative) by recognizing it as an affiliated body with the right to elect delegates to Zionist conventions.

Within Reform circles the inroads of Zionism were more dramatic. Signs of a shift from the classical anti-Zionism of Isaac Mayer Wise were apparent in the 1920s when Reform leaders, their fears of an imminent Jewish state allayed, cooperated in the economic upbuilding of Palestine. With the onset of Nazi rule they worked even harder to rehabilitate Palestine as a haven for refugees. In 1935 the Central Conference of American Rabbis formally revised early Reform views on Zionism, which had been formulated in the Pittsburgh Platform of 1885. Outright denial of Jewish peoplehood and the aspiration for a state now gave way to a resolution affirming the right of individual rabbis to choose their own stand on Zionism. Two years later both the CCAR and the organization of Reform lay leaders recognized the obligation of all Jews to cooperate in making Palestine a Jewish homeland—which they defined as a cultural and spiritual center. Reform Judaism's "conversion" was brought about in large measure by a change in its membership; those of East European descent were slowly outnumbering the German element.[4] More important, its faith in universalism and rational progress appeared increasingly unrealistic in an age of totalitarianism.

Totalitarianism also created a pro-Palestine orientation among the major Jewish labor groups. More and more unions contributed to the campaign drives on behalf of workers in Palestine, through which they were brought to a greater appreciation of that country's growth. The Jewish Labor Committee, a coordinating body of different unions set up in 1934, dealt with problems caused by nazism and discrimination in the United

States. It remained officially neutral on Zionism until 1947, but Zionists were able to build up their strength through its constituent units. In labor ideology, too, universalism, in the form of Marx's message to the working class, was eclipsed by a growing national consciousness.

No American Jew questioned the need for Palestine as a refuge. At a special nonpartisan conference called in 1935 by representatives of all types of Jewish organizations, claiming a combined constituency of 1,300,000 members, non-Zionists and Zionists pledged their support of co-operative efforts for rebuilding the land. The pressure of world events dictated unity, and Zionists fashioned their tactics accordingly. Restrained and cautious, they banished talk of statehood and independence. In that way they were able to avoid ideological rifts and, at the same time, find allies for their philanthropic campaigns.

Zionist groups supplemented general fund-raising with specific relief projects in Palestine. Hadassah found positions in its medical units for German Jewish physicians; Pioneer Women (Poale Zion) supported an agricultural school for the training of German girls; Mizrachi women raised special funds for Orthodox refugees. All those ventures contributed to the relief of German Jews and simultaneously to the growth of the Yishuv.

The most famous relief project initiated by Zionists was Youth Aliyah. Its director and inspirational symbol was Henrietta Szold, a woman then in her seventies. She was born in Baltimore, the daughter of a prominent Conservative rabbi. A humble but eminently talented and well-read young woman, she came to Zionism through her home and her reading, her love of things Jewish, and her admiration for Emma Lazarus. She worked for a while as secretary of the FAZ, and during the Brandeis era she directed the education department of the organization. Her most famous achievement was the founding of a young women's study circle out of which sprang Hadassah. Miss Szold's tireless devotion to that organization carried her back and forth between Palestine and the United States after World War I. Through Youth Aliyah the childless spinster became a substitute mother to thousands of refugee children. Her memory was permanently enshrined in the annals of the Yishuv.

Youth Aliyah originated as a plan to send German adolescents to Palestine and train them, culturally and vocationally, for a new life there. Primarily a rescue enterprise, it also promised to enrich the Yishuv with a particularly desirable age group. The program necessitated a highly complex organization and the cooperation of diverse groups: Jewish organizations in Germany for outfitting the emigrants, settlements in Palestine to which the children were sent for training, and the British government for the granting of special visas. Each phase of the program—from the escape out of Germany which became extremely perilous by 1938, to the integration of the individual child in Palestinian society—was a moving drama. Between 1934 and 1939, Youth Aliyah succeeded in settling over thirteen thousand children in Palestine. This twentieth-century children's crusade evoked a sympathetic response from Jewish communities throughout the world. In the United States Hadassah made Youth Aliyah its special project and by 1942 had raised close to four million dollars on its behalf.

IV

While the Zionist organizations worked for Palestine, the Zionist-oriented American Jewish Congress concentrated on defense activities. Like other defense agencies it looked for effective responses to the problems of German persecution, refugees, and the increasing anti-Semitism in Austria, Poland, and Rumania. It too published reports of discrimination and atrocities, and along with non-Zionists, leaders of the American Jewish Congress repeatedly made their way to Washington to plead the Jewish case. However, the American Jewish Congress also employed tactics different from those of the non-Zionists. Following its traditional preference for mass action, it organized numerous rallies and protest meetings, often with the support of prominent non-Jews. In 1934, it joined the American Federation of Labor in sponsoring a rally at Madison Square Garden at which it presented, in courtroom fashion, "The Case of Civilization vs. Hitlerism." The congress also became a staunch supporter of a public boycott of German goods. It discounted the fears of more cautious elements that such devices could boomerang and actually increase anti-Semitism. In so doing it provided a catharsis for those who wanted to stand up as Jews and sought to dispel the image of the cringing Jew. But its tactics neither ameliorated the situation of German Jewry nor goaded the Roosevelt administration into taking substantive action.

The plight of European Jewry elicited little more than polite sympathy from the administration. President Roosevelt, the internationalist who had run for vice-president in 1920 on a pro-League platform, and Secretary of State Cordell Hull, the spokesman of international free trade, followed the temper of the country. American isolationism grew stronger and more bitter during the thirties in the wake of the depression and the slow disintegration of the Versailles system. Public opinion considered America's involvement in World War I a mistake, if not a deception perpetrated by bankers and munitions manufacturers. From 1934 on, Congress worked at legislating a course of neutrality that would make similar involvement in another war impossible. Given this climate, the State Department easily decided that Nazi persecution was purely a German domestic affair which did not permit interference or even warrant representation on humanitarian grounds. In Congress resolutions for executive action could not get past committees. Jewish defense groups chose to blame Hull for America's silence rather than Roosevelt. Unfortunately their moral exhortation—"It is inconceivable that the American Government should stand passively by and neglect to lift its voice against these assaults upon humanity . . ." [5] —went unheeded.

The alarming rise in anti-Semitism in the United States led to other activities by the Jewish defense organizations. They all worked on multiple fronts, from private investigations of Nazi-type groups to vast educational campaigns stressing the ideals of brotherhood and democracy. For the most part they operated independently, but the severity of the crisis forced several short-lived attempts at unity.

The defense organizations tried to balance their concern over domestic anti-Semitism with their anti-Nazi or German-relief strategy. Jewish activity had to be so planned, they believed, that it would in no way evoke a backlash or be construed by the public as justifying the Jew-baiters. Moderation was the watchword, particularly with respect to securing a refuge in the United States for victims of the Nazis. Anti-immigration sentiment, hardened into law during the 1920s, increased during the depression. Its spokesmen combined economic arguments with nativist and racist beliefs when they proposed further cuts in the established quotas. American consuls abroad so tightened administrative procedures for prospective immigrants that only a small fraction of the quotas was filled. If immigration restrictions were relaxed for Jewish refugees, officials in Washington warned, anti-Semitism in the United States would certainly increase.

Doubtless that fear, reinforced by a desire to maintain a strong alliance with American labor on the issues of nazism and Palestine, was paramount in inhibiting Jewish organizations, Zionist and non-Zionist alike, from attempting to bring about a change in the immigration laws. They petitioned quietly for relaxation of consular procedure, and they fought congressional bills seeking to reduce quotas. But since they saw no chance in widening the quotas, they were reduced to a mere holding action. Caution on this matter contrasted sharply with the numerous public resolutions demanding that England open wide the doors of Palestine. Unfortunately, the world's refusal to accommodate the refugees helped thwart Hitler's original scheme to force the Jews to emigrate and contributed thereby to the extermination of millions.

V

During the years 1935–39, international events continued to underscore Jewish helplessness and public indifference. The Hitler regime had not collapsed or grown weaker, as some wishful thinkers had predicted in 1933, but had followed its consolidation within Germany by moves toward world conquest—the Rhineland in 1936, Austria and the Sudetenland in 1938, Czechoslovakia in 1939. The situation of the Jews grew progressively worse under the Nuremberg Laws of 1935. After Kristallnacht [6] in 1938 Germany unleashed a program of destruction and physical violence against Jews. Some two years later plans were laid for the "final solution," the extermination of European Jewry. Meantime, Nazi advances in Central Europe threatened the existence of many other Jewish communities.

The world made little effort to alter the sequence of events. The League, a pitiful caricature of Wilson's grand design, had already proved its impotence in the face of Japan's invasion of Manchuria and Italy's conquest of Ethiopia. Its half-hearted sop to those who pleaded the cause of the Nazi victims was the creation in 1934 of a Commission on Refugees, a private body supported by private funds and in no way part of League machinery, to service both Jews and non-Jews. An American, James G. McDonald, headed the agency for two years. His plans for negotiating with Berlin on behalf of systematic emigration and for working out schemes with other governments for large-scale resettlement failed. Ignored by Germany and rebuffed by refusals to admit refugees, he summed up the position of the Jews in bitter words: "[The] world has become disagreeably conscious of the Jews; they are considered a drug on the market." [7]

McDonald had envisioned Palestine as a major haven for Jewish refugees. Indeed, since most nations kept their doors closed, an increasing number of those who were able to flee Nazi rule and East European anti-Semitism made their way to Palestine. Immigration of Jews rose from ninety-five hundred in 1932 to over thirty thousand in 1933, forty-two thousand in 1934, and sixty-one thousand in 1935. Complex ordinances determined quotas for entry, but for the most part immigration was linked to the economic principle of the land's absorptive capacity. Meantime, Zionist groups in the United States wrote resolutions and petitions repeatedly urging Britain to facilitate the flow of immigrants into Palestine and even Transjordan.

But even that refuge was threatened, for the Arabs, alarmed over the influx of Jews and incited by Axis funds and propaganda, took action. In 1936 they staged a general strike, riots, and even armed revolt. Their principal demand during six months of disturbances was that Jewish immigration be stopped. Since appeasement was the regnant policy in England, the future looked threatening.

When the British government appointed the Peel Commission to study the Palestine situation and simultaneously announced a drastic cut in immigration, American Zionists stepped up their pressure. The Pro-Palestine Federation, a Christian group composed of clergy, intellectuals, and public figures, which had been organized in 1931, was the first to protest. Senators and congressmen joined Jewish groups in public demands for the continuance of immigration. The ZOA appealed for League intercession on behalf of those desiring to enter Palestine. The American Christian Conference on Palestine, including such famous personalities as labor leader William Green and former ambassador James Gerard, informed the British government directly of its support of Zionism. Conspicuously missing from the chorus was the State Department. A department memorandum of December 1936 disclaimed any responsibility for protecting the Yishuv; and although Secretary Hull kept the American ambassador in London informed of Zionist arguments, the administration remained silent.

As in 1929, Zionists and their supporters blamed the ineptitude of the British administration for contributing to the problem. Zionist memoranda directed to the Peel Commission called on Britain to discharge its responsibilities as mandatory power in proper fashion. One such document, signed by several Zionist and Palestine-investment groups, also stressed the economic reasons for American interest in Palestine. It estimated that eighty-one million dollars in the form of investments and gifts had been sent from the United States to Palestine.

The report of the Peel Commission in 1937 came out with the startling recommendation for partition of Palestine. Admitting that the mandate was unworkable in light of the Arab-Jewish conflict, it suggested that two separate states be created. The British would remain in overall control of the area by retaining a territorial zone that was to include Jerusalem, Bethlehem, and the major seaports. Another, albeit less satisfactory, alternative called for the imposition of restrictions on Jewish landholding and the substitution of political for economic criteria in determining Jewish immigration.

Zionists in the United States attacked partition with bitterness and anger. "We are betrayed," said Wise; partition denies "the integrity of the historic concept of the Holy Land," said Lipsky; a violation of "obligations entered into in good faith and sanctioned by international law," said Israel Goldstein.[8] The Orthodox group, Mizrachi, called on congregations to protest the plan during the fast day commemorating the destruction of the Temple. Clearly, a state reduced in size to twenty percent of the area of Palestine was unacceptable. It would solve neither the economic problems nor national antagonisms within the region. It would serve, as Abba Hillel Silver said, merely to make the Jews an insecure minority.

The non-Zionists agreed that the proposed state was politically and economically unacceptable. The very idea of an independent state, which they rejected while they cooperated in the rehabilitation of the land, upset them. Arguing that the myriad of problems resulting from statehood would divide Jewry and drain off resources at a time when Jews had to fight nazism, they wanted all of Palestine to be kept open for refugees.

In Congress resolutions were introduced opposing partition and asserting that American acquiescence was necessary before such a plan could be adopted. The ZOA also insisted that in light of America's role in World War I and, more specifically, as a result of the treaty of 1924, the United States's consent was necessary to any alteration in the status of Palestine. Britain denied the right of an American veto, but although the administration did not accept the British reasoning in full, it would not yield to congressional or Zionist pressure. It held fast to the narrow view of concern exclusively for "American" interests.

American Zionists reluctantly accepted the decision of the World Zionist Congress not to reject partition but to use the plan as a base for further negotiations with the British and the Arabs. The latter, however, expressed their uncompromising hostility to partition with open rebellion in Palestine beginning in 1937. In light of this development England backtracked and abandoned the scheme.

Zionist satisfaction was short-lived, for the events of 1938 brought new dangers and disappointments. Britain and France bowed to Hitler's design for conquest and his dismemberment of Czechoslovakia by signing the Munich Pact. The Nazis followed up Kristallnacht with new atrocities against Jews in Germany and Austria. In Evian, France, an international conference on refugees declined to hear discussion on Palestine as a possible haven, and meantime Britain refused to admit ten thousand refugee children into Palestine. Since the Evian conference failed to offer any constructive ideas on the refugee problem, the plight of European Jewry grew progressively worse and the need to keep Palestine open, more desperate.

When, in the fall of 1938, rumors circulated that Britain was planning to repudiate the Balfour Declaration and halt immigration in its entirety, Zionists and non-Zionists closed ranks in a campaign to mobilize American public opinion. They aroused clergymen, civic leaders, government officials, and educators to join in appeals and resolutions. Protest meetings were held throughout the country; the press responded sympathetically and asked England to meet its obligations. A delegation of Jews representing various organizations called on the British ambassador and pleaded for the right of immigration. Since the Jewish groups and their sympathizers also pressed for American intervention against a change in policy, Secretary Hull was constrained to make a public statement. He repeated the stock theme of America's interest in Palestine, but he carefully limited that interest according to the narrow interpretation of the 1924 treaty.

In May 1939 the fears of the Jews were confirmed. Britain issued a White Paper which announced the objective of an independent Palestine after ten years. It limited Jewish immigration to seventy-five thousand—ten thousand annually for five years and an additional twenty-five thousand refugees. Land sales to Jews were restricted, and measures were outlined for halting illegal immigration. Since authorized immigration was to stop as of May 1944, Jews in Palestine would never number more than a minority.

Denounced in England's Parliament and by the Permanent Mandates Commission of the League, the White Paper was also severely criticized in the United States. Senator Robert F. Wagner called it "Palestine's Munich." [9] The unity of Zionists and non-Zionists was reinforced, and again, allies in the form of the press, Christian clergy, and congressmen supported the Jewish case. Humanitarian needs had infused the Zionist cause with greater drawing power than ever before.

5

Herzl Reaffirmed

I

Unlike the situation that prevailed during World War I, Jewish sentiments were never in doubt after September 1939, when England and France finally awakened to the evils of Hitlerism. True, England was the author and executor of the White Paper, which cut off the one significant avenue of escape for European Jewry, and which the Jewish Agency termed "a breach of faith" in which "the Jewish people will not acquiesce." [1] But the fight against nazism, so long a purely Jewish cause, outweighed all other considerations. Chaim Weizmann pledged the loyalty of the Yishuv to Prime Minister Chamberlain even prior to the onset of hostilities. In the United States before Pearl Harbor, Zionists, like other Jews, openly supported the Allied cause.

Those Jews, however, who believed that waging a war on Germany would increase the sensitivity of the democracies to the specific plight of the Jews were doomed to disappointment. Perhaps just because Jewish loyalty could be taken for granted, leaving the Jews without any bargaining power, the attitude of callous indifference persisted. Britain, bent on wooing the Arabs, adhered strictly to the White Paper. The United States refused to take action, although members of Congress agreed with the Zionist contention that the White Paper repudiated the Balfour Declaration and the terms of the mandate, and violated the Anglo-American treaty of 1924. Roosevelt was primarily concerned with the need to stop Hitler, but in 1939 he faced a Congress that was reluctant to abandon its isolationist posture and a country whose mood was expressed in the words: "We'll sit this one out." [2] Although the president privately questioned why England was reneging on its obligations, he feared that anti-British statements would strengthen the isolationist camp. Thus, at the same time that the United States was arguing the sanctity of international agreements to the Axis countries, it refrained from using the same arguments against England.

Officially, the State Department followed its narrow interpretation of the 1924 treaty: American responsibility extended solely to the limited interests of American nationals in Palestine. Logically, that line of reasoning might have led to official action. The American Jewish Committee pointedly asked the State Department whether American Jews would fall under the immigration restrictions of the White Paper. The question really meant that since American non-Jews were unaffected, would the United States permit a foreign government to discriminate against its citizens on grounds of religion? The State Department dodged the issue. It admitted that American Jews were subject to the restrictions, but it thought the problem academic, since in time of war there would be no available transportation to Palestine for anyone!

The United States also followed England on the matter of a Jewish fighting force. That plan was originally broached at the beginning of the war by Zionist leaders who proposed that a separate Jewish unit be set up within the British army. Aside from any political advantages that might accrue thereby in Palestine, the unit could serve in the Middle East in the event of Axis attacks. But, although Palestinian Jews served in the British forces, political considerations and appeasement of the Arabs prevented the formation of an official Jewish brigade until the end of 1944.

During the course of the war the idea of a broader Jewish army, including Jews from other countries, took shape. Differences of opinion among Jews were expressed as to its size, under whose command it would fight, and where it would serve, but in all its forms the idea derived from, and in turn enhanced, the concept of Jewish nationalism. Its spokesmen shared common assumptions. Since the Jews as a people were the special target of the Nazis, a Jewish army would provide them with the means to combat their enemy directly. An army denoted peoplehood, if not a claim to sovereignty, and by contributing to the Nazi defeat it could strengthen the bargaining position of the Jews at the end of the war.

In the United States the Jewish army idea, under Revisionist and Revisionist-like auspices, proved especially appealing.[3] Assisted by Ben Hecht, a journalist and playwright whose identification as a Jew came as a reaction to nazism, the militants ran a colorful publicity campaign calling for an independent army recruited from Palestinian and stateless Jews. The Zionist establishment denounced the scheme, for it ran counter to the policies of the World Zionist Organization, and it was primarily aimed at strengthening the militants' position within the Yishuv. Nevertheless, their flamboyant propaganda—playing upon emotions of courage and righteous anger—drew support from Jews who had shown scant interest in Zionism. Cabinet officials and Chief Justice Harlan Stone also added their endorsements. But the militants failed to secure the assistance of Congress and the White House, for the State Department warned that agitation for an army was having harmful effects on Arab relations with the United States.

Stymied by the British on the issues of immigration and a military force, the Yishuv took matters into its own hands. The popular slogan of the day—"to fight the White Paper as if there were no war, and to fight Hitler as if there were no White Paper"[4]—was difficult to live by. Pressure for noncooperation with the British abated during the war years, but the Yishuv was fashioning an administrative structure which would steer it on the course to independence. In accordance with its policy of active opposition to the White Paper, it expanded the Haganah, and it organized illegal immigration into Palestine.

Illegal immigrants—persons without British visas—had arrived in Palestine even before 1939. Then, when European Jews were trapped between Nazi brutality and the quota cuts of the White Paper, their number increased. The World Zionist Congress openly supported illegal immigration, for humanitarian considerations did not shake Britain's determination to bar the refugees. The latter were hunted down and even fired upon. Those who were apprehended were deported or interned, and officials deducted the estimated number of those who succeeded in entering from the regular annual quotas. (The American labor Zionist magazine, *Jewish Frontier,* commented: "Were Britain as faithful to its international obligations as . . . to its self created . . . policy in Palestine, the world would appear different today.")[5] Meantime, Palestinian Jews evaded British searchlights, police boats, and secret agents in their struggle to smuggle in refugees. Jews throughout the world were generally sympathetic, agreeing with an American Zionist leader who said that to talk of illegal immigration at that time was immoral.

British policy gave Zionists in the United States a weapon for mustering support against the White Paper. Public opinion was particularly aroused after the *Struma* incident. That ship left Rumania for Palestine in December 1941 with over 750 refugees, none with immigration permits. It broke down off Istanbul, but Turkish authorities would not permit the passengers to land without British visas. The British refused, and a few weeks later the ship was ordered to leave despite its unseaworthy condition. It sank a few miles from shore, and all but two passengers were drowned.

Zionist frustrations sharpened in intensity when news of the Nazi extermination camps reached the free world in 1942. Deportations of Jews, walled-off ghettos, and mass shootings had been reported since the German invasion of Poland. But the Nazis now sported new weapons to expedite the "final solution" of the Jewish question: gas chambers within the concentration camps and Zyklon B gas to be used on the inmates.

Ever since 1933 the logic of Nazi ideology and policies had pointed to extermination, but civilized society was incredulous. Despite a war which unleashed new weapons of destruction, systematic extermination of a civilian group could not be fathomed. The evidence mounted, but the Roosevelt administration was not moved to initiate rescue attempts. Special prayers, protest meetings, and appeals to the White House were of little avail. Some suggested bombing the camps or giving the inmates prisoner-of-war status; others advised the establishment of underground railroads. Those ideas too were fruitless.

At a conference in Bermuda called by Britain and the United States in 1943, the plight of the Jews was buried in a discussion of the overall refugee problem. A special memorandum from the major American Jewish organizations appealed for negotiations with Germany for the release of Jews, the designation of havens of refuge, the liberalization. of American quota laws, and the entry of immigrants into Palestine. But the conference denied admittance to Jewish representatives. Their memorandum was not considered, and Palestine was not even mentioned as a possible haven. The unavailability of shipping to transport refugees was raised as a major obstacle to rescue endeavors.

The United States was no less guilty than Britain. It kept silent from 1939 to 1942 despite news of increasing Nazi barbarity, and out of an exaggerated fear of subversives it tightened administrative procedures for refugees seeking entry into the United States. At Bermuda the American immigration system was also beyond the pale of discussion. Roosevelt's Secretary of the Treasury, Henry Morgenthau, has told in his diaries how American officials suppressed the first news of extermination—the State Department even convinced the American Zionist leaders to go along in that move—and turned away from specific rescue attempts which offered good chances of success. A report prepared for Morgenthau on the situation was bluntly entitled "Report to the Secretary on the Acquiescence of This Government in the Murder of the Jews." [6] At Morgenthau's prodding the administration finally set up the War Refugee Board in 1944 "to take all measures within its power to rescue the victims of enemy oppression who are in imminent danger of death." [7] However, the move was too little and too late to effect any notable achievements.

James MacGregor Burns, in his biography of Roosevelt, concludes that the main reason for the absence of forthright action on the president's part was his war strategy. The only way to rescue the Jews would have been negotiations with the Germans, a policy which Roosevelt judged to be contrary to the doctrine of unconditional surrender. That left the fate of the Jews dependent on whether the Allies could defeat Hitler ahead of the timetables of the gas chambers.

If rescue action was not forthcoming, how much more impossible was it to expect any disinterested sympathy with Zionism? By the middle of the war American Jews and their organizations realized that specific Jewish needs were not included in the general struggle against Hitler, that victory would not automatically right the Jewish situation or advance Jewish aspirations. As Congressman Emanuel Celler put it, by the time victory came the Jews trapped by the Nazis would have been exterminated.

II

The full meaning of the Holocaust did not hit American Jewry until after the war. Their initial incredulity gave way to a kind of numbness, an inability to digest the impersonal casualty statistics, which mounted higher and higher. Only when they learned of relatives who had perished, when they saw army films of the extermination camps or, worse still, the bars of soap or lampshades made from Jewish bodies, did they begin to grasp the magnitude of their loss. Six million Jews had been done to death, while the world stood by. Slowly they began to realize how the United States, like the other major powers, and Roosevelt, like other heads of state, shared in the responsibility for the tragedy.

Some Zionists had questioned even earlier the belief that Roosevelt was the devoted friend of the Jews. From their vantage point the president was at best a silent sympathizer, more likely a double-talking politician who kept the Jews in line with glib promises. Since the Nazi terrors had changed Zionism from a mere nationalist movement into the rescue channel for European Jews, Roosevelt was morally guilty for withholding his support. Not until 1944 did he voice disapproval of the White Paper, and not until the campaign of that year did he pledge support to a Jewish commonwealth.

Such criticism, in the light of the domestic and international realities of the thirties, appears overly simplistic. What is more significant is that it could not shake the equally naive faith of American Jews in Roosevelt. A passionate loyalty to the president and the New Deal was shared by most Zionists and non-Zionists. They saw Roosevelt as the omnipotent champion of the common man, the protector of the insecure and the not-quite-accepted. The president's stand on Zionism was less important, but they could build up his image on that level by pointing to his friendship with Stephen Wise and Felix Frankfurter. During the war the president was consistently cordial and sympathetic when he was visited by Dr. Weizmann and American Zionist leaders. Members of Roosevelt's administration and of Congress also told the Zionists that they could count on the president.

Until the middle of the war Zionists refrained from actively pressuring the administration. That tactic was later challenged, leading to a serious rift within Zionist ranks. But both to those who counseled moderation and those who preached agitation, Roosevelt was the key figure in solving the Palestine situation. Wartime diplomacy was summit diplomacy; at conferences of heads of state, plans were being blocked out for the postwar world as well as for the conduct of the war. Since the United States now had a direct stake in the Middle East through the Middle East Supply Center and the lend-lease program, it would in all likelihood no longer abdicate responsibility over that area to the British. American aid would be indispensable whether Zionists hoped to pressure England into a liberal mandate policy or sought to bypass England in favor of an alternate political system for Palestine. Perhaps, too, Roosevelt's anticolonial posture, which he adopted on occasion with Churchill, might be used to reinforce Jewish nationalist claims. Thus, as long as Roosevelt made American foreign policy, his assistance was vital for furthering Zionist aims.

Both Roosevelt and the State Department sought to avoid commitments on the Palestine problem. The government had no overall Middle East policy, much less specific plans for the fate of Palestine. Indeed, only with the advent of the war did the area assume major significance in American diplomatic calculations. Its strategic importance was primary; gateway to three continents, the Middle East was also the corridor for transporting supplies to Russia. Its oil resources enhanced its attractiveness. Not only was the government determined to protect the concessions held by private American companies, but by 1943 a deep concern over the need for petroleum during and after the war led the government to formulate plans for direct American entry into the Middle East oil business. It was imperative, therefore, to keep the Arabs from joining the Axis. In its efforts to cultivate friendly relations, the United States sent lend-lease supplies and other forms of economic aid to Saudi Arabia.

Expanding American activity in the area led to a certain amount of rivalry with the British, who were jealous for their own prestige and oil interests. Secretary Hull's tentative long-range goals for the Middle East, including eventual independence for the various countries and their participation in the United Nations, were also questioned by England. The State Department avoided additional contention by refusing to take a position on the questions of Jewish immigration into Palestine and of a Jewish state, which it regarded as exclusively British concerns. In the interests of wartime unity it appeared safer to suspend discussion on the postwar status of the Middle East. According to Hull, pressure by American Jews and counterpressure from the Arabs, the military, and consular officials forced the president to talk "both ways to Zionists and Arabs." But "[the] State Department made no pledges." [8]

While his administration was busy reassuring Arab leaders every time the Zionists secured a favorable statement from a public figure, Roosevelt straddled the issue. In the first years of the war, when the Axis threat to the Middle East was gravest, he avoided any moves which might have conflicted with British policy or incited the Arabs. After Rommel's forces were halted, other considerations dictated soft-pedaling the Zionist issue. Churchill advised that the question be postponed until after the war, and only concerted pressure by Zionist leaders forestalled an Anglo-American statement suspending deliberations entirely. American officials, many of whom were pro-Arab, stressed to the president the United States' dependence on Middle Eastern oil. Moreover, if Russia planned to support the Arabs after the war, as reported to Roosevelt by Averell Harriman, pro-Zionist acts by the United States might antagonize Stalin's government and jeopardize the success of the United Nations. These factors built up what some Zionists called the government's "conspiracy of silence," which reached its peak in 1942–43.

For a time Roosevelt hoped for a rapprochement between the Jews and the Arabs. That hope had been entertained into the thirties by the Zionists themselves. They thought that the economic benefits brought about by Jewish settlement and shared by the Arabs would make the latter look favorably upon Jewish immigration and the development of a Jewish home. Roosevelt counted on charming King Ibn Saud, even as he had Joseph Stalin, into cooperating. One specific plan discussed briefly by Roosevelt,

Churchill, and Weizmann was put forth by H. St. John Philby, a British adviser to Ibn Saud. It contemplated leaving Palestine to the Jews in exchange for a monetary grant to Ibn Saud and British and American support of Arab independence in all other Middle East countries. That scheme fell through, and Roosevelt admitted the futility of bringing about a negotiated settlement between Arabs and Jews after his meeting with Ibn Saud in 1945.

Next, Roosevelt considered the idea of making Palestine a religious trusteeship under the supervision of representatives of the three faiths, but that too was quickly abandoned. What exactly Roosevelt meant by still another remark, that at the end of the war the United Nations would have to create a commonwealth in Palestine, is not known.

Contradictions beclouded Roosevelt's very last comments regarding Palestine. According to a statement which Stephen Wise was authorized to release after an interview in March 1945, Roosevelt reaffirmed his 1944 pledge of assistance to the creation of a Jewish state. Yet a few days later, at a meeting with two executives of the non-Zionist American Jewish Committee, the president reportedly stated that a Jewish state would, under present conditions, be impossible to achieve; furthermore, he said he had told Wise that Zionist agitation for a state would cause grave disturbances in Palestine and might even create a situation that could lead to a third world war. At the same time, but unknown to the Jews, Roosevelt repeated his assurance to Ibn Saud that he, Roosevelt, would do nothing hostile to Arab interests.

One thing was certain. Roosevelt had promised the Arab king that Arabs and Jews would have the opportunity to express their views before a definitive decision was reached, and in that way he had acknowledged the United States' obligation to participate in resolving the future of Palestine.

III

Until America entered the war Zionists were generally silent about their aims for a postwar Palestine. In addition to their sympathy with the British fight against nazism, they realized that the isolationists, whose stance was anti-British, would feed on other anti-British activities.

Fear of anti-Semitism also inhibited American Jewry from calling for any international involvement. Attacks on Jews as warmongers increased between 1939 and 1941, for Jews had been conspicuously anti-Nazi since 1933. Jew-baiters and Nazi sympathizers joined the isolationist ranks and lent an anti-Semitic flavor to the cause. The America First Committee, which spearheaded the isolationist sentiment in the foreign policy debate on intervention, was not an anti-Semitic organization, but it received the endorsements of Coughlin and Pelley. When Charles Lindburgh, speaking for the America First Committee in 1941, announced that the "three most important groups who have been pressing this country to war are the British, the Jewish and the Roosevelt administration," [9] he articulated a widely held view.

Zionist visitors to the United States commented on the inertia of the Jewish community. Rabbi Solomon Goldman, president of the ZOA from 1939 to 1941, also attacked what he called the paralyzing timidity of the American Jews. The latter were too engrossed in anti-Semitism, too apologetic, too amenable to counsels of self-negation or silence on Palestine. Denouncing the argument that Jews must step aside since larger issues were involved, Goldman called for unremitting efforts on behalf of a Jewish homeland in Palestine.

A fearful or apathetic community was not the proper repository for world leadership of the Zionist movement. Yet, as in World War I, the helplessness of European Jewry and the isolation of the Yishuv dictated that American Jewry exercise increased initiative. When Dr. Weizmann visited the United States at the beginning of 1940 he told his audiences that the double task of making policy and providing support for Palestine had fallen on them. After Pearl Harbor the major deterrent to American Jewish activity was removed. To state the demands of Zionism in unequivocal terms, to make Zionism a mass movement coterminous with the American Jewish community, and to win general American support for the Zionist cause became the goals of American Zionism.

The new goals involved a radical departure in both the content and the form of American Zionism. Most important of all, the Zionists revived the Herzlian message—the demand for a Jewish state. At the time of the Balfour Declaration a Jewish home in Palestine was generally interpreted to mean a state. However, in the 1920s it was watered down to signify a spiritual or cultural center, and in the 1930s it meant a haven of refuge. For many years independent statehood as a tangible goal for European and American Zionists had been excised from the Zionist vocabulary and program. Under Weizmann's leadership the tone of the world organization matched its words. It was moderate, conciliatory, anxious to cooperate with the mandatory power and the Arabs, eager to placate the Jewish anti-statists. But after the war broke out, the plight of European Jewry, coupled with Britain's intransigence and America's silence, forced the movement to a more militant posture.

During 1941 the word *commonwealth* gradually replaced *home* when Zionists in the United States talked about Palestine. At the sessions of the National Conference for Palestine, the nonpartisan fund-raising agency, Rabbi Silver said in simple fashion: "We have no new aims. . . . Our aim is a Jewish Commonwealth." [10] House Majority Leader John McCormack echoed the hope for a state, and the conference went on record in favor of a Jewish commonwealth. Zionist leaders Weizmann and Ben-Gurion, on visits to America, repeated the term on other occasions. Later that year the ZOA resolved more forcefully: "We solemnly declare that the rapid resettlement and rehabilitation of the homeless Jewish masses can be effected only by the reconstitution of Palestine, in its historic boundaries, as a Jewish Commonwealth." [11] As the *Jewish Frontier* editorialized, the growing ferment indicated that the Zionists would no longer be satisfied merely with some vague declaration.

At a special Zionist conference held in May 1942 at New York's Biltmore Hotel, the change in terminology became fixed Zionist policy. The meeting, attended by more than six hundred delegates from all parts of the country, symbolized the shift in leadership to the United States. Weizmann and other European Zionists participated, giving the gathering the semblance of a World Zionist Congress, the highest policy-making body of the Zionist movement. Indeed, only after the conference took its stand did the World Zionist Organization approve the new emphasis in program. The Jewish Agency, based in Jerusalem, also acknowledged the primacy of the United States and American Jewry in Zionist diplomacy when, in 1943, it established an office of its political department in Washington.

The resolutions passed by the conference and known thereafter as the Biltmore Program set the Zionist sights on goals which in reality were only a reaffirmation of Herzl's original platform. They insisted on mass immigration into Palestine in order that a Jewish majority in a democratic commonwealth be assured.

> The Conference calls for the fulfillment of the original purpose of the Balfour Declaration and the Mandate which *"recognizing the historical connection of the Jewish people with Palestine"* was to afford them the opportunity, as stated by President Wilson, to found there a Jewish Commonwealth. . . . The Conference urges that the gates of Palestine be opened; that the Jewish Agency be vested with control of immigration into Palestine and with the necessary authority for upbuilding the country, including the development of its unoccupied and uncultivated

lands; and that Palestine be established as a Jewish Commonwealth integrated in the structure of the new democratic world.[12]

The Zionists did not go on to discuss how they intended to carry out their aims. There was no talk, for example, of dropping the mandate. Yet the Biltmore Program was not empty rhetoric. It gave American Zionism a new lease on life which transcended the political goal. The *New Palestine,* supporting the "need for militancy," [13] saw it as a step in recovering the missionary zeal of the early Zionists and in using Zionism to restore Jewish self-respect.

The demand for a commonwealth was but one strand of a revitalized American Zionist program. To wield any appreciable influence Zionists needed to show that they spoke for American Jews at large. During World War I they had organized the American Jewish Congress with the hope that it would become the recognized voice of the community. Now, in anticipation of major international changes at the end of the war, they again worked for unity. Their call struck a responsive chord, for many Jews, seeking efficiency and group strength in time of emergency, deplored the multiplicity of communal organizations.

Unity in fund-raising for Palestine was reached in 1941 after many years of interorganizational bickering. The United Jewish Appeal, which represented the major philanthropic causes, collected larger and larger sums during the war years. In 1945 American Jewry's contribution reached thirty-five million dollars. The share for Palestine grew as the volume expanded, and, in addition, the very percentage allocated to Palestine rose. But Zionism benefited in more ways than financial. In the light of world events Zionists did not have to dilute their goal of statehood, as they had in the 1920s, to corral the assistance of the usually non-Zionist financial establishment. Zionists were also able to utilize fund-raising devices, such as dinners and conferences, to spread support for their goals. As the contributions spiraled, they could claim, and with justification, that they had the backing of the community. Moreover, unity in philanthropy set a pattern of cooperation which would lead to unity in political action.

The very logic of fund-raising went still further. The reality of a vibrant Yishuv of six hundred thousand Jews committed to the ideal of independence could not be denied. To extend economic aid, to stimulate cultural enterprises, or to facilitate the flow of immigration automatically strengthened the goals of that Yishuv. The non-Zionist middle-of-the-road position, which usually signified support of Palestine but repudiation of political nationalism, had lost its meaning. In effect, even in their response to philanthropic drives, American Jews were taking a stand on Jewish nationalist aspirations.

Dr Weizmann took a further step toward unity in 1941 when he inaugurated a series of conferences between Zionist representatives and the American Jewish Committee to explore areas of agreement. If a rapprochement could be effected with the committee, whose prestigious members wielded great power in Jewish defense and fund-raising, the Zionists would have scored a notable coup. For a while it appeared that a formula would be worked out by which the committee would agree to a Jewish state if the Zionists renounced the concept of diaspora nationalism. But the anti-Zionists on the committee won out, denouncing Jewish statehood and the Biltmore Program. In 1943 the organization resolved to support a United Nations trusteeship over Palestine at the end of the war.

Zionism encountered more vicious opposition with the organization in 1942 of the American Council for Judaism. Founded by the anti-Zionist rabbis of the CCAR who were defeated on the Zionist issue in that body, it launched an all-out attack on Jewish nationalism. Its ideology echoed the universalistic platform of nineteenth-century Reform, which it coupled with charges of dual loyalty against the Zionists. Its appeal, as reflected in a survey of its leadership, was mainly to upper-class Reform Jews of German (ethnic) origin. While it opposed the White Paper for denying equal rights to Jews, it labored energetically to counter Zionist pressure on the American government and Zionist influence within American society. The first and only organization dedicated expressly to fight Zionism, it proved most useful to Christian and Arab anti-Zionists. Zionists were constrained to divert energy and funds to combat what they termed the council's "treason." Special committees on unity for Palestine were formed and thousands of pieces of literature were distributed in that effort. The council, whose numbers came to no more than two percent of Zionist membership, provided Zionism with a target against which to sharpen its own crusade.

Despite the critics and detractors, Zionists labored to mobilize the community behind the Biltmore Program. Plans were laid for creating an American Jewish Conference, composed of the national Jewish organizations, for the purpose of dealing with the postwar needs and status of Jews and the question of Palestine. In Zionist calculations the conference would serve to show both the unity of American Jewry and its commitment to the Zionist idea. Public pressure in open sessions might also convince non-Zionist groups like the American Jewish Committee to cooperate in the interests of maintaining their position within the community. In 1943, through a complicated electoral process, delegates representing close to half of America's five million Jews were chosen by communities throughout the country. Zionists successfully campaigned for the election of their partisans, and the adoption of a system of bloc voting for the sessions further strengthened their control over the vast majority of votes. The final decision rested with the Zionists—either to push for endorsement of the Biltmore Program or to hedge on statehood and avoid any split within Jewish ranks. Led by Abba Hillel Silver and abetted by his skillful rhetoric, the maximalists triumphed over the moderates. The conference officially backed the reconstitution of Palestine as a Jewish commonwealth by a vote of 478 to 4. Not all of the constituent bodies of the conference followed suit—the American Jewish Committee, in fact, broke away just because of the Palestine resolution—but the loud public support mustered by the resolution launched the conference to an auspicious start.

IV

The note of militancy expressed in the Biltmore Program and reinforced by the American Jewish Conference also colored Zionist tactics. To claim the backing of most American Jews (i.e., of most of those who chose to identify as Jews) was not enough, and Zionists set out to transform the community into an active political force. Emanuel Neumann, a prominent ZOA executive, described the task in the following way:

> This involved a radical change of attitude, a transvaluation of values. . . . Our people had to learn to become vocal and articulate, politically active and mobile. They had to be taught how to rally about them a host of Christian friends. . . . Above all, American Jews and American Zionists had to become politically alert and mature, to distinguish between words and deeds, between promise and performance, between gracious messages and pronouncements from Washington designed for home consumption and actual political effort and diplomatic assistance on the part of the American Government. . . . American Zionists had to be braced to engage in a serious political struggle and to employ in that struggle all the legitimate means available to free men in a free society.[14]

In 1939, in recognition of American Jewry's leadership in time of war, a coordinating agency, the Emergency Committee for Zionist Affairs (ECZA), was set up to join the ZOA, Hadassah, Mizrachi, and Poale Zion for the purpose of spreading the Zionist message to the American people. Neumann headed its public-relations campaign and was successful in establishing two groups for channeling Christian support of Zionism. One, the American Palestine Committee, was headed by Senator Robert F. Wagner of New York, a liberal and a staunch supporter of the New Deal. Even critics of Zionism admitted that Wagner was prompted not by political motives but by a genuine sympathy with Zionism. The senator kept in close contact with Neumann, particularly with regard to enrolling senatorial support. By the end of the war the American Palestine Committee claimed a membership of sixty-five hundred, many of whom were outstanding public figures. The second, the Christian Conference on Palestine, one of whose founders was theologian Reinhold Niebuhr, consisted entirely of clergymen. In 1945 it numbered twenty-four hundred. The two Christian groups merged that year into the American Christian Palestine Committee.

Neumann and others were disappointed, however, over the ECZA's political passivity. Many within the community deplored the lack of leadership, which was comparable to that exercised by the Brandeis team of World War I. Soon after the establishment of the American Jewish Conference the agency was reorganized as the American Zionist Emergency Council (AZEC) under the joint chairmanship of Stephen S. Wise and Abba Hillel Silver. It was Silver who sparked a change in tactics. Impressive in bearing, an impassioned orator, and a forceful leader, Silver was a prominent Reform rabbi of Cleveland who had been active in Zionist work since the start of his career. He had left the ZOA with the Brandeis faction in 1921 and, unlike Wise, did not return to a position of leadership for many years. Uncompromising in his demand for a Jewish state, he stood for political agitation, convinced that the United States would behave in pro-Zionist fashion only under public pressure. His views brought him into conflict with Arab sympathizers, the State Department, and even some prominent Zionists. The Wise-Lipsky leadership, entrenched for years and loyal to the Weizmann line, had grown moderate and cautious. Wise, a personal friend of Franklin Delano Roosevelt and a loyal Democratic campaigner, counseled against challenging the administration. Silver was nineteen years younger, untouched by the tradition of conciliation, and a Republican. He never enjoyed Roosevelt's friendship the way Wise did, but his leadership attested to a shift within the Jewish community. Just as Ben-Gurion signified the growing militancy of the world Zionist movement away from the Weizmann tradition, Silver was the symbol in the United States of Jewish impatience with the American Zionist establishment.

The AZEC embarked on an expanded program, setting up an office in Washington and new departments to handle problems of public relations and postwar planning. In addition to frequent press releases and purchases of radio time, it promoted the publication and distribution of vast quantities of literature geared to America's opinion-molders. Works by non-Jews were particularly significant; Dr. Walter C. Lowdermilk's book, *Palestine: Land of Promise,* which dwelt on the potential of the land's productivity, made the best-seller list. The AZEC also strengthened ties with Christian groups, and it made special efforts to mobilize support from the academic community, heretofore consistently cool or apathetic toward Zionism. Zionists bypassed the neutralist Jewish Labor Committee, and with the organization in 1944 of the American Jewish Trade Union Committee for Palestine were able to obtain significant backing from Jewish and non-Jewish labor. The absence of organized anti-Zionism on the part of the Christian spokesmen or the oil interests facilitated the operations of the AZEC. In fact, the critics of Zionism whom the AZEC fought were Jews—notably the Revisionists and the American Council for Judaism.

The AZEC's most important tactical move was the establishment of over four hundred local emergency committees. The latter were charged with the tasks of establishing contact with politicians of both parties and working for the expression of pro-Zionist opinions by municipal and state bodies. The committees were also taught how to run publicity campaigns to arouse public opinion, and they built up techniques of petitions and letter-writing drives for making that opinion known in Washington. Through these means national Jewish opinion was heard in favor of the abrogation of the White Paper and the establishment of a Jewish commonwealth.

The non-Jewish public voiced its approval, too. State legislatures in 1944 and 1945 passed resolutions supporting a Jewish commonwealth. Prominent figures in government, labor, the churches, education, and the arts gave their individual endorsements. Their stand was more than a response to Zionist pressure; basically, it reflected horror over the Nazi atrocities and sympathy with the needs of the survivors. Support from non-Jews in turn reinforced the Zionist convictions of the Jewish community.

For a while it appeared as if the Zionists would succeed in their ultimate aim: to force the administration, under public pressure, to adopt a policy in support of Zionism. Arab and British spokesmen had complained in 1941 about the American Palestine Committee—which included scores of senators, congressmen, and governors—since they feared it would be interpreted as an official American commitment. The State Department sympathized but could not curb the APC. In August 1943 Congressman Emanuel Celler wrote an open letter to the president accusing State Depart-

ment officials of encouraging Britain to violate its obligations. He intended
to ask for a congressional inquiry into the activities of three department officials, Patrick Hurley, Wallace Murray, and Harold Hoskins, unless the department ceased its opposition to Palestine as a haven for Jewish refugees.
By the end of that year the AZEC ascertained that a majority in Congress
were prepared to support a pro-Zionist resolution. Sponsored by James
Wright and Ranult Compton in the House and by Wagner and Taft in the
Senate, resolutions were introduced at the beginning of 1944 which stated:

> That the United States shall use its good offices and take appropriate
> measures to the end that the doors of Palestine shall be opened for free
> entry of Jews into that country, and that there shall be full opportunity
> for colonization so that the Jewish people may ultimately reconstitute
> Palestine as a free and democratic Jewish commonwealth.[15]

The State Department quietly opposed the resolution, even though it
would not have been binding on the executive. According to Hull, its passage could incite conflict in Palestine, imperil American oil interests, and
stimulate others to press for similar resolutions on areas like Poland and
Italy.

The Zionists who testified before the House Committee on Foreign Affairs built their case primarily on historical and humanitarian grounds. They
also stressed the accomplishments of the Yishuv and the rights and advantages which the Arab population would enjoy in a democratic state controlled by a Jewish majority. Rabbi Silver pointed out that in view of their
recent experiences, Jews could no longer rely on promises of a brave, new
postwar world. He claimed that appeasement of the Arabs was unnecessary,
that the case of North Africa, where the United States supported the restoration of Jewish rights in the French territories captured by the Allies,
proved that a show of force caused no outbreaks. Only one Zionist wit-
ness, Professor Carl Friedrich of Harvard, came close to arguing that support of a Jewish state was in the best interests of the United States. Other-
wise the Zionist testimony rested on the needs and rights of the Jews and
not on America's diplomatic concerns.

The House committee heard opposing testimony from Arab sympathizers and from the American Council for Judaism, but there was no
doubt of its own pro-Zionist sentiments. Nevertheless, in response to a note
from Secretary of War Stimson advising that his department considered the
resolution "prejudicial to the successful prosecution of the war," [16] the
House committee and the Senate Committee on Foreign Relations decided

against taking action. Congress, public opinion, and a well-organized lobbying group could not override the executive.

The Zionists determined to continue their pressure for congressional action as soon as the military situation allowed. Meanwhile they had to be content with a statement from Roosevelt in March 1944 to Silver and Wise.

The President has authorized us to say that the American Government has never given its approval to the White Paper of 1939. The President expressed his conviction that when future decisions are reached, full justice will be done to those who seek a Jewish National Home, for which our Government and the American people have always had the deepest sympathy. . . .[17]

Strictly speaking, "never given its approval" did not mean that it disapproved; nor did "National Home" mean commonwealth. But coming as it did on the eve of the expiration of Jewish immigration into Palestine, the statement marked the first time that the United States publicly diverged from Britain's mandate policy. In Silver's opinion, Zionist agitation had brought about the statement, which finally broke the "conspiracy of silence." However, a follow-up request from Wise and Silver for an unequivocal presidential endorsement of a Jewish commonwealth did not receive a reply.

Asserting that they were not committed to either major political party, Zionists could store up political capital for what it was worth during an election year. Both the Republicans and the Democrats, against the better judgment of Secretary Hull, wooed the Zionists with platform planks endorsing unrestricted immigration and the creation of a commonwealth in Palestine. The Republicans, whose isolationist old guard still delighted in anti-British jabs, also condemned Roosevelt for failing to insist that Britain live up to its obligations. Despite protests from the Arabs and the American Council for Judaism, candidates Roosevelt and Dewey added their personal endorsements. Roosevelt promised more than he ever had:

I know how long and ardently the Jewish people have worked and prayed for the establishment of Palestine as a free and democratic Jewish Commonwealth. I am convinced that the American people give their support to this aim; and, if re-elected, I will help bring about its realization.[18]

Silver worked to offset the lulling effect which the president's words might have on the Zionists. In a speech a few days later he insisted that Zionists continue to mobilize public opinion, which in turn would force official action. "Put not your faith in princes," he intoned, but "talk to the whole of America." [19]

On a go-ahead sign from Secretary Stimson in October the sponsors of the congressional resolution renewed their efforts. After the election the House committee favorably reported the resolution, albeit in somewhat diluted form, but action by the Senate committee was blocked on the advice of the president and the State Department. This defeat for the Zionists caused a split within their ranks. The Wise faction charged that Silver's group had violated an AZEC decision in pressing for the resolution without securing prior approval from the administration. Furthermore, since the Wise faction had informed Washington that it was not pushing the resolution, Silver's conduct exposed Zionist disunity, tarnished the Zionist public image, and needlessly antagonized the administration. The World Zionist Organization agreed with Wise. The episode resulted in Silver's resignation, forcing the Jewish community to debate the issue of moderation versus agitation. When public clamor brought about Silver's reinstatement less than a year later, it proved again the widespread support for an activist line.

Despite their successes in mobilizing public opinion, American Zionists could not convert the Roosevelt administration to a pro-Zionist position. In the last analysis the Zionist movement of the war years had its greatest success within the Jewish community. World events between 1939 and 1945, particularly the extermination camps, predisposed the Jews to respond to the appeal of Zionism. The multiple propaganda themes employed by the Zionists were effective in reaching different kinds of Jews on various grounds and in reinforcing that predisposition. Nor were American Jews held back by the fear of anti-Semitism, even though polls continued to report high indices of prejudice. After Pearl Harbor, at least in the circles of opinion-molders, anti-Semitism—an enemy device and contrary to the democratic ideals of the war—became increasingly less respectable.

By 1945 the ZOA claimed over 136,000 members (compared to 8,900 in 1933); the total number of Zionists of all parties was some 400,000. Membership statistics told only a small part of the story. Stephen Wise boasted that if the commonwealth resolution passed by the American Jewish Conference were submitted to a referendum, it would muster the approval of ninety to ninety-five percent of American Jews. His estimate was largely vindicated by a poll in 1945 which reported that only ten percent of American Jews opposed a Jewish state in Palestine.

The mood of the community was changing, too. Time and time again the rank and file pushed the organizations to more militant action. The leaders could not have stopped the commonwealth resolution of the American Jewish Conference; the local emergency committees of the AZEC pressured the central office to greater agitation; the rank and file overrode the moderates and forced Silver's reinstatement. As the community grew more assertive so did the Jewish establishment. After the first steps taken during the war years, American Jews grew accustomed to arguing their claims with self-assurance, no longer behaving in accord with the wishes of the administration. The Holocaust had taught them that Christian society would not respond to the gravest of crises. Jews, therefore, could count only on themselves to further Jewish interests.

6

The Rebirth of Israel

The horrors of Nazi genocide echoed long after V-E day. The once populous Jewish communities of Europe, if not completely obliterated, were physically decimated and left bereft of schools, synagogues, and other cultural resources. Over two hundred thousand Jews remained interned in refugee camps. Spared from the gas chambers by the Nazi defeat, they were destitute, homeless, and, for various reasons, nonrepatriable. And the legacy of Nazi anti-Semitism, woven into the social and legal fabric of the former Axis countries and their satellites, minimized the chances for Jewish recovery and security.

American Jewish defense organizations took on the problems let loose by the Nazi whirlwind. Preparation of briefs against war criminals, demands for reparations from Germany, measures for immediate relief of the displaced persons, insistence that rights for Jews be incorporated into peace treaties with the former enemy nations—in all these major activities, singly and together, they participated. Shaken by the magnitude of the Holocaust, they realized that the Allied victory alone, or the post–World War I formula of minority rights, or even the establishment of the United Nations with an international bill of rights, was not sufficient. Upon the Jews themselves rested the principal burden of salvaging whatever future remained for their people in Europe.

No longer were American Jews merely sympathetic but detached philanthropists; they were personally involved. There was scarcely a Jewish family in America without a relative or friend who had died at the hands of the Nazis. The community as a whole sustained a collective loss, since East European Jewry, the cultural reservoir of the Jews of the New World since the eighteenth century, had literally been bled dry. Perhaps most unsettling was the realization that the gas chambers were earmarked for the

Jew irrespective of citizenship. The victims might have been they themselves.

The emotional reaction to the Holocaust and to the plight of the survivors strengthened the Zionist cause, adding to it new dimensions of passion and vigor. Whether supporters saw a Jewish state as the only solution for the DPs, or as a guilt offering for the six million victims, or as a touchstone for Jewish survival in an alien world, Zionism offered a broad enough base to absorb varying motivations. In addition, there were no longer any reasons of wartime expediency to warrant restraint or silence. Financial contributions and membership figures continued to rise after 1945. In 1948 there were over 711,000 enrolled in the major Zionist parties (compared to 387,000 in 1945), and in that year American Jews contributed more than ninety million dollars for Palestine. Eliezer Kaplan, treasurer of the Jewish Agency, wrote to his colleagues in Palestine about the spirit of devotion which, aside from vast contributions, characterized American Jewry after the war: "I should also tell you of the growing sense of Jewish solidarity and of the widespread readiness to take part in the struggle for our national future. This is in fact the message I was asked to convey to you at all kinds of gatherings, of labour and middle-class circles, of Zionists and non-Zionists, of young and old alike." [1] Non-Jewish Zionist sentiments grew stronger too, particularly through the efforts of the American Christian Palestine Committee.

Despite overwhelming public support, Zionists were able to present their case only unofficially to the delegates at the San Francisco conference for launching the United Nations in April 1945. As Dr. Israel Goldstein, co-chairman of the American Jewish Conference, pointed out: "It was a vicious circle. [The Jewish people] had no status there; therefore they could get no status." [2] At San Francisco the Zionists gained no more than a decision *not* to alter their rights under the mandate. For the next three years they continued to look to the Big Three, particularly the United States, for the creation of a Jewish state in Palestine.

I

The end of hostilities in Europe and in the Pacific signaled the emergence of new diplomatic problems for the United States. The Grand Alliance, as Churchill termed the wartime coalition of Russia, Britain, and the United States, barely survived through 1945. Signs of impending conflict were brushed aside by the pressures of military strategy or, at the end of the war, by the desire of the American people for rapid demobilization. But by 1946 the cleavage between Russia and the West led Churchill to talk of an "Iron Curtain"; in 1947 Bernard Baruch coined the phrase "Cold War." Meantime, an exhausted Britain could no longer shoulder its traditional responsibilities in the Middle East and eastern Mediterranean. When the Soviet Union put pressure on Turkey and Greece in 1947, only the United States could offer effective resistance. Its response was the Truman Doctrine. From then on the administration continued to formulate policies according to the guidelines of containment—a policy which led the United States to assume direct and ongoing responsibilities for the maintenance of world order.

Against that background the Palestine problem had become knottier. In addition to the legacy of conflicting pledges made by England to the Arabs and the Jews, and the growth of the Jewish settlement in Palestine, there was now the factor of Palestine as part of the Middle East, an area whose strategic importance and oil resources required that it remain out of Soviet hands.

Harry S. Truman did not inherit any substantive policy from his predecessor with regard to Palestine. Personally he was sympathetic to Zionism, attracted as a believing Christian to the religious imagery surrounding Zion. He also viewed the Zionist movement as an expression of self-determination of nationalities, one of Woodrow Wilson's "noble policies." [3] But harsh realities beclouded idealism. Zionism had become a serious issue in domestic politics, and partisan pressures on the question of a Jewish state confronted him as soon as he took office. While congressional opinion was markedly pro-Zionist, even on the part of members without Jewish constituencies, the State and War departments were most concerned about the feelings and threats of the Arab governments as they bore upon American interests in the Middle East. In their calculations the needs of the containment policy were of primary importance. Caught between conflicting demands, Truman, like Roosevelt, was led to attempts at pacifying both sides.

In light of the historical background of the Arab-Jewish impasse, it was difficult to see how any solution, or even a continuing policy of no solution, would be accepted peaceably by all. But Truman sought an answer that would neither incite violence in the area nor require the use of American troops for its implementation. Genuinely concerned about the plight of the DPs, he would have liked to see them admitted to the United States and other Western lands. Congress, on the other hand, firmly objected to a relaxation of immigration restrictions. Since the DPs were welcome nowhere but in the Yishuv, to which their entry was barred by the White Paper, the refugee issue overlay the Palestine problem. Truman, however, tried to keep the two questions separate, insisting that the matter of a state should be handled by the United Nations. Until Britain formally announced its intention to terminate the mandate in 1948, he was reluctant to commit the United States to any responsibility in carrying out decisions about Palestine. Truman's position, therefore, was not likely to satisfy the Arab sympathizers, the impatient Zionists, or the harried British.

Until the fall of 1946 Truman supported immigration into Palestine as distinct from statehood. More concerned than his State Department about the suffering Jews in Europe, he commissioned Earl G. Harrison, dean of the University of Pennsylvania Law School, to report on the DPs with special reference to the Jewish refugees in Germany and Austria. Harrison disclosed the horrible conditions in the camps, and he depicted the particularly grim existence of the Jews. Stressing the need for quick evacuation, he recommended that one hundred thousand be admitted into Palestine. Even before he received Harrison's report, Truman, against the judgment of the State Department, prodded Churchill and Attlee at the Potsdam conference of the Big Three to relax the immigration restrictions. He then took up the plea for one hundred thousand despite the fact that the Zionists and the British both insisted that the totality of the Palestine situation be faced. The British desired an American commitment to help shoulder the burden of possible resettlement, and the Zionists argued for the immediate establishment of a state. England agreed to the entry of fifteen hundred a month, but American Zionists greeted that action with scorn.

When, in October 1945, British Foreign Minister Ernest Bevin proposed a joint Anglo-American Committee of Inquiry on the Palestine question, American Zionists called the move a stalling device. They interpreted America's consent to the proposal as a sign of yielding to British policy. Their fears mounted when the president, who had at first supported a congressional resolution on Zionism, announced that he no longer favored that move. The Zionists derived scant satisfaction from the slate of Americans chosen by the president to serve on the committee, for, with the exception of James McDonald, the appointees were not known to be sympathetic toward Zionism or even conversant with the issues. Zionist apprehensions were borne out by the committee's report. True, it called for the immediate admission of one hundred thousand refugees into Palestine and the removal of restrictions on land sales and transfers. Nevertheless, insofar as it rejected the idea of a Jewish state and proposed a United Nations trusteeship preparatory to a binational state, the report spelled regression to the

American Zionists. Repudiation of the White Paper of 1939 had come too late; Zionists would not bargain for less than a state.

Richard Crossman, a Labour member of Parliament who served on the Anglo-American committee, observed the American Zionists when they testified before that body. Initially Crossman considered them an unsympathetic lot—noisy, argumentative, unbending in their indictment of Britain for having contributed, with the White Paper, to the death of countless Jews. They were "absentee Zionists," who would not consider substituting Palestinian for American citizenship. But Crossman's personal aversions were modified when he grasped the mood of American Zionists in 1946. He was particularly impressed by Dr. Emanuel Neumann, the adroit legal mind, and by Rabbi Stephen Wise, who "speaks and looks like the prophet Micah." [4] Their insistence on Palestine was not motivated by selfish desires to keep Jewish refugees out of the United States. If Congress permitted, they would have gladly welcomed the DPs. Even the absentee Zionists displayed a genuine passion for their cause, and, like all Jews outside Palestine in the aftermath of nazism, a feeling of separateness and homelessness.

The anti-British hostility reported by Crossman signified a change from the pre-Pearl Harbor days when American Jews were among England's staunchest supporters. The Zionists' grievances against England intensified when the Labour government, faced with severe postwar burdens and diplomatic pressures, repudiated its original pro-Zionist position. Before its victory at the polls Labour had called for the abrogation of the White Paper, unlimited Jewish immigration, extension of Palestinian territory, and even Arab resettlement. Once in office the Labour government proceeded to handle the Palestine problem with a remarkable degree of ineptitude. The more the British stalled, the more they encouraged the extremist elements among the Arabs and Jews. Justifiably irritated by the United States' penchant for giving advice without constructive assistance, they refused to heed the humanitarian demands on behalf of the DPs. That in turn strengthened the Zionist resolve to expand the system of illegal immigration. The British responded with internment camps on Cyprus for illegal immigrants—a striking reminder of Nazi concentration camps. These policies aroused widespread terrorist activities within Palestine, which in turn led to heavy British military reinforcements, a virtual siege of the Yishuv (June 1946), and suppression of the Jewish Agency. The crackdown on Zionists, which automatically meant tipping the scales toward the Arabs, appeared singularly grotesque after a war in which the Arabs had collaborated with the Axis and the Palestinian Jews had supplied troops for the British.

England and the United States drew no closer after the Committee of Inquiry submitted its report. Truman backed the recommendation for one hundred thousand immigrants into Palestine but reserved judgment on the ultimate disposition of the country. Prime Minister Attlee maintained that the report as a whole would have to be considered and that the one hundred thousand could not be admitted until the terrorists were completely suppressed. Foreign Minister Bevin added a gratuitous insult when he said that America's insistence on the one hundred thousand derived from the fact that it did not want too many of those immigrants in New York. Bevin's statement may have been true, but his undiplomatic words drew protests from both Jews and non-Jews. Silver accused him of a "cheap slur on the American people, and a coarse bit of anti-Semitic vulgarity"; [5] New York's senators, Wagner and Mead, protested directly to Bevin about his insulting and Nazi-like words. When England refused visas to Palestine for Wise and Lipsky, American Zionists were further offended. Because of these acts it appeared for a while as if England would not secure the loan it requested of the United States. To reduce the strain between the two countries and work out a joint program on Palestine on the basis of the committee's report, Truman appointed a cabinet committee to negotiate with their British counterparts. The United States now offered to transport the one hundred thousand to Palestine and share in the costs of resettlement.

II

American Zionists meantime continued their stepped-up pressure tactics along the lines they had set during the war. Now their activities were encountering greater resistance, for the Arab League established its own office in Washington in 1945. Zionists distributed vast quantities of literature and held mass demonstrations in support of a Jewish state and in opposition to the Labour government's policies. With the strong backing of Senators Wagner and Taft they finally succeeded, in December 1945, in securing a congressional resolution upholding Jewish immigration into Palestine and the development of Palestine as the Jewish national home. Weaker than the original version in that it did not speak of a Jewish commonwealth, the measure circumvented the president by being passed as a concurrent resolution.

Although in theory Zionists rejected the idea that a Jewish state was justified solely as a means to absorb refugees, they gained widespread sup-

port within the community just because nothing had been done to evacuate
the European camps. American Jews hailed Truman's pronouncements on
DPs, but they chafed at the administration's inaction. In July 1946 a unique
type of protest was staged. Four thousand American Jewish war veterans
marched on Washington demanding implementation of the one-hundred-
thousand proposal. If the United States needed troops to help carry it out,
they were ready, they said, to raise two divisions of Jewish ex-servicemen
for that purpose.

American Jews increasingly identified with the Yishuv in its resistance
to British immigration policies. Stephen Wise, a moderate, wrote to a
Christian friend in 1946:

> My people would not be worth their salt if they were ready to remain
> out of Palestine because of a White Paper or because the English have
> decided that they may enter Palestine only with certificates. That the
> Jewish people should practice non-violence in a Christian world of
> violence is asking too much of those who have suffered most in the
> war and who are more truly homeless than any group on earth.[6]

Since Zionist sentiment had become so widespread, the leaders of the
Yishuv were able to bypass the organizational framework and appeal to
American Jews directly. At a private session with a select group of wealthy
American Jews in 1945, David Ben-Gurion discussed the financial needs
of his countrymen entailed in the rescue of the DPs and the struggle for
independence. Out of that meeting was born the "American section of
Haganah," which, in quiet operations across the country, raised eleven
million dollars and procured guns, planes, and ammunition for the Yishuv.
It also bought ships and engaged crews for Haganah's Aliyah Bet (illegal
immigration) activities. Ten such ships, manned by American crews, ran
the British blockade to land their cargoes of European refugees on Palestinian shores. The Americans who enlisted in Haganah work were of varied
backgrounds—many non-Zionist, some non-Jewish. In their wide range of
operations they were forced to dodge embargo regulations, Arab agents,
and police and FBI surveillance. When it became known that England
would give up the mandate in May 1948, they raced against time to prepare the Yishuv for facing the Arab nations alone.

The report of the second Anglo-American committee, the Morrison-
Grady plan, further strengthened American Jewish unity. Proposing a division of Palestine into three parts under overall British trusteeship—the
area of the Jewish canton to be less than sixty percent of what the British
had suggested in 1937—the plan made the admission of the one hundred

thousand contingent upon the adoption of the entire proposal. Zionists, non-Zionists, and even the American Council for Judaism protested, pointing out again how the DPs were the unhappy victims of diplomatic bickering. The long-range solution aroused the Zionists and also drew criticism from the American advisers to the committee, the members of the first Anglo-American committee, influential congressmen, and Democratic party leaders. Clearly the British-inspired proposals were not, as they were to have been, the means to implement the recommendations of the first committee. Secretary of State Byrnes, eager for Anglo-American accord in the Middle East as a counterweight to Russia, approved the Morrison-Grady plan. Truman, who was showing signs of impatience with Jewish and non-Jewish critics, was also inclined to agree. However, when he realized that Morrison-Grady was totally unacceptable to both Arabs and Jews, and promised further violence, he yielded to the opposition and rejected the scheme.

The Morrison-Grady fiasco had far-reaching results. In the first place, it showed that Truman's attempts to separate the refugee issue from consideration of the final disposition of Palestine were increasingly unworkable. Secondly, failure to secure action on the DPs brought the last important non-Zionist stronghold, the American Jewish Committee, to the side of statehood. Thirdly, the breakdown of Anglo-American negotiations prompted the Jewish Agency to put forth an idea of its own.

Dr. Nahum Goldmann, a member of the executive of the Jewish Agency, arrived in Washington at the beginning of August 1946 to present the agency's plan for the partition of Palestine into an Arab and a Jewish state. According to Goldmann, the agency had no other choice. It feared that England was bound to take drastic action sooner or later against the Yishuv's terrorist and immigrant-smuggling operations, and that incessant attacks by American Jews on the State Department and England would lead to a serious rupture between Great Britain and the United States. David Niles, assistant to Truman on minority groups, had warned the agency that if no reasonable plan were forthcoming, the president would wash his hands of the entire affair. To continue the mandate or to establish another transitory regime with the hope of gaining a Jewish majority within a limited time period were unrealistic prospects. Equally impossible was a demand for all of Palestine as long as Jews constituted a minority. Reluctantly, therefore, the agency decided on partition, an immediate and practical solution.

Partition had another advantage. The United States had no alternative

plan when Truman rejected Morrison-Grady, and Byrnes reportedly
would have nothing further to do with the issue. It was likely, therefore,
that if presented with a plan which claimed to have Zionist and British
acceptance, the administration would be receptive. Goldmann secured the
approval of Under-Secretary of State Acheson, Secretary of the Treasury
Snyder, and Secretary of War Patterson. Niles and Acheson were to talk
to the president.

Goldmann found an influential ally in Joseph M. Proskauer, president of the American Jewish Committee. The leader of the anti-Zionist faction within the committee, which had helped wreck the negotiations with
the Zionists in 1942, Proskauer supported the admission of one hundred
thousand to Palestine while continuing to oppose a Jewish state. Since
1943 the committee had stood for a trusteeship in Palestine where Jewish
immigration and land settlement would be limited only by the economic
principle of absorptive capacity. Although Proskauer specifically rejected
partition when he testified earlier in 1946 before the Anglo-American
Committee of Inquiry, the hopeless situation of the DPs and the fear of
never-ending guerrilla warfare in Palestine made him amenable to the
agency's plan. When both Secretary Patterson and Under-Secretary Acheson gave their endorsements, and when Acheson added that Proskauer
personally could render valuable service by his support, Proskauer was
convinced. The American Jewish Committee was brought about to favor
partition and a Jewish state not as an ideal choice but as the course most
likely to obviate greater evils.

Ironically, the Zionists were the ones to find fault with the agency's
move. They had long opposed partition in principle, and they bitterly attacked the agency's repudiation of the Biltmore Program. The ZOA in convention talked of "the whole of mandated Palestine"; the Mizrachi pointed
to Torah-ordained "historic boundaries." [7] Silver and his followers de-.
nounced the partition plan at the World Zionist Congress in December
1946. It was, they charged, an error in judgment and in tactics. It left
Zionists with an "irreducible minimum," [8] bereft of any bargaining power.
Those who continued to uphold the classic Zionist position were now considered extremists.

The American government did not adopt the policy as its own; nor
did the sacrifice on the part of the agency evoke a well-intentioned coun-
teroffer from England. At the Zionist congress the Silver faction defeated
the Weizmann-Wise group, which was willing to negotiate with England on
some form of partition. The congress established an American section of

the Jewish Agency under Silver's chairmanship, and Wise, whose affiliation with the Zionist movement had spanned half a century, announced that he was leaving the ZOA. Zionist moderation had fallen before American Jewish militancy.

Goldmann related that Truman's approval of the agency scheme was secured on August 9. In a public statement on October 4 Truman referred to that plan. Though careful not to adopt it as the government's, nor to commit himself to its specific terms, he said:

> [It] is my belief that a solution along these lines would command the support of public opinion in the United States. I cannot believe that the gap between the proposals which have been put forward [Morrison-Grady and Jewish Agency] is too great to be bridged by men of reason and good will. To such a solution our Government could give its support.[9]

Truman's statement evoked anger and threats from the Arab countries. To Ibn Saud the president defended his remarks, asserting America's responsibilities to the DPs and to the creation of a Jewish national home in Palestine. He didn't think, he added, that those sentiments represented "action hostile to the Arab people." [10]

The Jewish Agency recognized that Truman had given only tentative and qualified approval to their plan. The American press, however, highlighted the story as presidential support of a Jewish state. James Reston of the *New York Times* wrote that Truman had flouted his advisers with the statement, which was clearly the product of domestic political pressures. Anti-Zionists latched on to that line to explain all moves by the government in support of a Jewish state from 1946 to 1948. Nevertheless, theirs was an oversimplification, even a distortion, of Truman's policy.

Dean Acheson, an anti-Zionist and Truman's under-secretary of state, has most recently denied that the October statement was a political maneuver. True, it was released on Yom Kippur eve and was timed with the November elections in mind—particularly the vote in New York, Pennsylvania, Illinois, and Ohio. Zionists had worked for it in line with the precedent established in 1944 of seeking support from both major parties. Democratic politicians used it to offset Republican counterbids. But the essence of the message was no different from what Truman had said before. He was still concerned about the DPs, whose fate hung in the balance. He sought a solution for Palestine that would stabilize the region, a prime objective in light of the Cold War and containment. A proposal like Morrison-Grady only invited resistance by all sides. If a scheme like the agency's could gain the consent of the various protagonists—and neither the White House nor the British believed at this time that the Arabs would resort to open warfare—it was worth considering. (Even Byrnes and Acheson chose partition when Lord Inverchapel, the British ambassador, theorized about three possible courses: partition, United Nations assumption of the mandate, Morrison-Grady.) However, only four months later, when conferences between England and the Arabs failed to win Arab agreement to partition or even a modification of Morrison-Grady, Truman admitted that he was as far from a solution as ever.

III

When England asked the United Nations in February 1947 to take up the Palestine issue, it was not yet prepared to surrender the mandate. The British only wanted an opinion on how to administer the land. Bevin blamed his government's failure to resolve the problem on the United States and the American Jews, who, he charged, undercut the British by their games of domestic politics. The British move accorded with Truman's view of United Nations responsibility, but in an international undertaking the United States would now be forced to shoulder some responsibility for Palestine's future.

After a year and a half in office the Labour government had little to show for its costly program of maintaining order in Palestine. Arab and Jew were united only in anti-British sentiments; terror mounted in the Yishuv despite the British police state. The more England warred with the Yishuv, the greater the pressure by the Zionists upon the United States. While England was motivated principally by the desire to keep Arab friendship, the United States still had no overall policy on Palestine. The lack of initiative on the part of the two Western powers lowered their prestige, and the impasse strained Anglo-American amity.

A special session of the General Assembly convened in April 1947 at which time a United Nations Special Committee on Palestine (UNSCOP) of eleven "neutral" nations was appointed to investigate the problem. Despite pressures from American Zionists and their sympathizers in Congress, the United States adopted a studiedly impartial attitude and refused to prejudice UNSCOP's deliberations with its own suggestions. Senator Robert Wagner received no response when he pleaded that the State Department publish the documents in its possession on the Arab-Axis nexus.

The involvement of the United Nations and creation of UNSCOP increased tension in the Yishuv and further exacerbated Anglo-Zionist relations. Britain was no longer the mediator between contending factions in Palestine but an active belligerent against the Jews. Haganah, the Yishuv's police force, could not keep the Jewish terrorist element in check. In the United States the Revisionists were conducting a boycott of British goods and services, and like their predecessors of 1768 named themselves the Sons of Liberty. Despite Truman's plea for restraint, the Jewish community continued its financial support of illegal immigration and terrorist groups. The British ambassador was driven to protest to the State Department when an advertisement in the form of a letter by Ben Hecht congratulated the Palestinian terrorists on their bombings and shootings of the British "invaders." When Congress debated aid to Greece and Turkey, Zionists suggested that the United States should back up British policy in those countries only in exchange for British approval of the admission of one hundred thousand to Palestine.

If the anti-British mood needed further stimulus, it was provided by the *Exodus* affair of July 1947. The *Exodus* was an American steamer purchased by the Haganah to transport refugees from Europe through the British blockade. Manned by Americans, it picked up its cargo—over forty-five hundred persons—at a southern French port and headed for Palestine. British ships intercepted it, and, after a struggle in which several on board were killed and many injured, escorted it to Haifa. There, for one day, the passengers were kept on the ship in cages. Instead of interning them in Cyprus, Britain decided to return the refugees to their port of origin, where they were brought aboard three British transports. Since the French would admit them only if they disembarked voluntarily, and since most of the refugees refused to budge, the British took them to Germany, where they were forcibly interned. Public outrage led the United States to urge London to reconsider its decision, but to no avail.

Shortly thereafter UNSCOP submitted its report. The majority called for the partition of Palestine into one Jewish and one Arab state, within an economic union, with Jerusalem under a United Nations trusteeship. Americans of both parties and of different political outlooks responded enthusiastically. So did the vast majority of American Jews. Rabbi Silver and his followers now supported partition, explaining that it had made no sense for Zionists to consider such a plan until it was broached officially to them. When UNSCOP began its deliberations, Silver, the representative of the Jewish Agency before the General Assembly, had appealed to the world organization to uphold the commitments of the Balfour Declaration and the mandate. Partition, Silver now told the General Assembly, meant an "enormous sacrifice," [11] for the proposed state was less than one-eighth the size of the original area covered by the Balfour Declaration. Nevertheless, the Zionists would accept and, he promised, were prepared to be good neighbors to the surrounding Arabs.

The position of the American government was uncertain. UNSCOP's report made a pro-Zionist policy easier to uphold. First, it proved to the cynics that Zionist claims had a validity that transcended American politics, and second, to deny the justification for a Jewish state was now a contradiction of a United Nations agency. But other factors made the United States hesitate.

A succinct summary of the interests that opposed a Jewish state has been provided by Professor Frank Manuel. (1) There were strategists concerned with military bases and oil supplies who strove to keep the Middle East quiescent and free of disturbances. A possible base for military operations against Russia, Palestine, with its harbors, Mediterranean coastline, proximity to Suez, and terrain suitable for use as airfields, was of particular value. Zionism aroused Arab resentment, and it would be folly to encourage a movement which bred discord, especially since the Arabs might then cut off the flow of oil. Besides, the Jews of the Yishuv, unlike the Arab fellahin, could not be so easily controlled by the West. (2) There were the Anglophiles in the State Department, emotionally attached to the policy of cooperation with England. If the United States continued to regard England as a vital force in the free world, it should oppose Zionism, which was working to force England to relinquish control over Palestine. (3) There were the missionaries and educators, well represented in the foreign service, who were jealous of their Christianizing influence among the Arabs and resentful of "alien" civilizations. (4) And there were the oil men, enjoying vast concessions from Arab rulers, who worried about their profits. Seeking government support for their operations, and encouraged by a government which needed their product, they opposed anything which might upset their relations with the Arab states.

United in a fundamental opposition to Zionism, these groups found more immediate arguments to use against partition. Since England rejected UNSCOP's report, implementation would depend on American-Soviet cooperation, a course for which the American public was not prepared. Besides, could the United States work against England when containment of Russia seemed to argue for the adoption of British policies in the Middle East? Arab nations warned of a third world war if the United States backed partition. Even if that threat was exaggerated, American action might alienate the Arab states, push them into the Soviet orbit, and weaken American influence with the Muslim world in the United Nations.

From September to November 1947 the General Assembly considered UNSCOP's report. The Zionist case was handled by a Jewish Agency delegation under the direction of Moshe Shertok, later Israel's minister of foreign affairs, whose political skill led America's General John Hilldring to comment: "Shertok could sell ice to the Eskimos." [12] Zionists found a strong supporter in Hilldring, adviser to the American delegation. Herschel V. Johnson, the American representative to the United Nations, originally thought of partition as a surrender to political pressure, but he soon became convinced of the rectitude of the Zionist cause.

American Zionists and their Christian allies aided the propartition endeavors by stepping up their pressure upon the administration. Two new weapons found their way into the campaign. A Jewish state was now justified by its supporters as fitting the primary aim of America's foreign policy, the protection of democracy against communism. A democratic state in the Middle East was important for American interests, and America's support, just like the Truman Doctrine and the European Recovery Program, would be a symbol of the nation's purpose as a world leader. The Zionists also benefited from Truman's friendship with his one-time business partner, Eddie Jacobson. Officers of B'nai B'rith prevailed upon the latter to speak to the president, and between June and November Jacobson presented the brief for a Jewish state personally to his friend in the White House.

On October 11, Herschel Johnson announced American support for the principle of partition. Basically, it was a compromise position, for the government yielded neither to those advisers who feared Arab reaction nor to those who favored a commitment to the use of force, if necessary, to implement partition. Nevertheless, the statement shocked both the Arabs and the British. On the other hand, it marked the first time that the United States and the Soviet Union were joined together in the United Nations on a major issue. The Russians, eager to displace Britain in the Middle East, temporarily gave up their traditional denunciation of Zionism and supported partition.

Once the principle of partition was recognized, the powers worked on the boundary question and on various aspects of implementation. With respect to boundaries, a personal visit by Weizmann to Truman saved the Negev, or southern part of Palestine, for the Jews. The United Nations also agreed to appoint a committee for preparing the two new states for independence, which would come about two months after Britain surrendered the mandate. However, since the United States was unalterably opposed to committing its troops or permitting Soviet troops into the area—and since the United Nations did not have its own constabulary force—the actual implementation of the partition decision rested on the acquiescence of the Jews and Arabs. Herschel Johnson's conviction that member states would not defy a United Nations decision helped to smooth the way for the final vote on partition.

When the blueprint had been fashioned, Johnson appealed more strongly for partition. He said that "the governments who believe in partition think that it is not perfect, but that it is humanly just and workable and if adopted will make a genuine and notable contribution to the solution of one of the most thorny political problems in the world today." [13] Zionists indulged in last-minute hectic lobbying to enlist the support of different national delegations. Whether the United States (and Truman himself) engaged directly in similar pressure has been disputed. One account explains that while the State Department decided to desist, David Niles was telling Johnson to apply pressure. On November 29 the General Assembly mustered the necessary two-thirds majority to pass the resolution providing for the partition of Palestine.

The charge (or claim) was made immediately, and has reverberated ever since, that the General Assembly's vote on partition was brought about by Zionist political pressure. Voiced by friends as well as foes of a Jewish state, it goes like this: (1) Despite American hesitancy about the merits of partition, Zionists, fortified by American Jewish voting strength in key urban areas and by Jewish financial contributions to the Democratic party, bypassed the State and Defense departments and forced a naive or vote-chasing Truman to support partition. (2) Prominent Jews and their sympathizers in government, and/or the government itself, pressured other countries—usually the list includes Haiti, Liberia, the Philippines, and Ethiopia—to cast their votes in favor of partition. The memoirs of Truman and his associates and of Zionist leaders abound with anecdotes on how key figures were approached. Primary and secondary accounts go on to evaluate the success or failure of specific episodes. The entire theme has been further developed by political analysts and ethnic historians to prove theories of bloc voting or the hyphenate in politics.

It cannot be denied that there was unremitting Zionist pressure, which annoyed officials, including the president, and that Truman acted at various times in opposition to members of the executive departments. But ethnic politics was only one determinant of the American position on Palestine. The president's overriding concerns in foreign affairs were to contain Russia and to uphold the United Nations. Other problems awaiting resolution were the DP situation and the warfare in Palestine. Insofar as a Jewish state could offer viable answers or serve his objectives, Truman would be amenable. He had no serious reason to fear the loss of Jewish political support. In 1944 American Jews had voted more solidly for the Democratic party than ever before. Conversely, if he were impelled solely by political considerations, Truman would have moved more swiftly and directly from 1945 on in the direction of a Jewish state. In fact, government reversals in policy *after* the partition vote (November 1947–May 1948), despite the approaching 1948 elections, and Truman's policies vis-à-vis Israel from May 1948 to November 1948, prove that political expediency was not the overriding motive.

Critics of Zionism have bitterly contended that the Zionists and their allies refused to heed the counsel of the State and Defense departments. In ruthless pursuit of their goal they brushed aside objective experts and selfishly bartered away American needs. Since the critics have postulated that a Jewish state was disadvantageous to the United States, those who pushed for it, up to and including Truman, were guilty of sacrificing their country's interests for their own narrow purposes.

Even if one agreed that the critics and the anti-Zionists in government were not anti-Semitic but motivated purely by the desire to protect American interests, one could still legitimately question their interpretation of national interest. There was no certainty that without the creation of Israel the Arabs would be loyal and friendly to the West. Despite England's restrictions on Zionists after 1937 the Arabs had continued to collaborate with the Axis. Besides, the Arabs wanted American money. In 1946 Truman's pro-Zionist statement caused Syria and Lebanon to threaten American companies. When the companies hinted that they might take their business elsewhere, the Arabs forgot their threats. Some strategists also counseled the government not to rely on Middle East resources, since their vulnerability to attack made them unreliable links in America's defense chain.

The case against Zionism admitted of no other policy for the promotion of America's best interests but the appeasement of the Arabs. Yet the only solution the Arabs would have accepted willingly was the creation of an independent, unitary state in Palestine, in which Jews, as a recognized minority, would, at best, enjoy some measure of municipal and cultural autonomy. From America's point of view that plan was untenable. It would have ended Jewish immigration into Palestine, a cause to which the United States had been committed since 1945; it would have required considerable force to impose, since the Jews were determined to fight for large-scale immigration; it probably would not have been approved by the United Nations, for it was not even close to UNSCOP's report. Given the fact that the British, Arabs, Jews, and United Nations agreed that the mandate had to end, partition offered the best prospect for a solution.

The charge that Zionist pressure was responsible for partition rested on two unwarranted assumptions: that the Jews of the United States wielded a tremendous power totally out of proportion to their numbers, and that the American Jewish community offered a monolithic political response to matters of Jewish interest. One may well ask at the very outset: If indeed those assumptions were true, why did the American Jews not force the government to save their European coreligionists from extermination?

American Jews constituted a bare three percent of the population. An urban, educated, and politically alert group, their votes could perhaps be pivotal in large cities, but only if they voted as a solid bloc on Jewish matters. But Jews, like other Americans, cast their ballots according to the dictates of their economic and social interests, the needs of their neighborhoods, cities, and states, and their national political loyalties—as well as in response to ethnic and religious factors. The evidence shows that in comparison with other ethnic minorities in the United States, the Jews have lagged behind in expressing group interests. Unlike the Irish and the Germans they organized few Jewish political clubs. Often they sought to play down or disavow concerns that set them apart from the American political mainstream. Jewish candidates could not count on support from their community simply because they were Jewish; in certain cases being Jewish was a liability in the eyes of the Jewish community. Politicians courted the Jewish vote, but that vote was not determined by Jewish interests alone, nor did it mean "winner take all."

American Jews have enjoyed no special political power, and their economic power has been grossly exaggerated. True, they have become an affluent group; their concentration in urban areas and white-collar positions have accounted for an income-level higher than that of most other groups. They have played important roles in the worlds of light industry, consumer products and services, and communications. But they were conspicuously absent from the development of heavy industry and, until very recently, virtually invisible in managerial echelons. The charge of Jewish power derived less from fact than from age-old popular reaction to the Jews—the "accursed race" which rejected Jesus but through mysterious powers was able to survive divine and man-made retribution.

The indictments against the Zionists for their activities during 1947–48—power politics, ruthless manipulation, lack of patriotism—echoed long-held anti-Jewish stereotypes, which in turn could become provocations for the incitement of virulent anti-Semitism. In this case the stereotypes were shifted from "all Jews" to Zionists. In light of the overwhelming endorsement of statehood by American Jews, the distinction lost meaning. Anti-Semitism at the end of the war was largely the trade of the radical right and the lunatic fringe, but it stood to regain respectability in the guise of anti-Zionism.

IV

Contemporary accounts of the reaction to the General Assembly's vote on partition record the jubilation with which it was greeted by American Jews. Nevertheless, apprehension soon replaced joy. Neighboring Arab states immediately began sending men and matériel to strengthen the Palestinian Arabs in their attacks against the Yishuv. Banking on the big-power rivalry to block enforcement of the United Nations decision, they determined to make good their threat to prevent the establishment of a Jewish state. An embargo imposed by the United States on arms to the Middle East was serving in fact as a punitive measure against the Jews, for the Arabs continued to receive military equipment from England. Moreover, Britain, which had long ceased to maintain order in the country, prevented the organization of an official Jewish militia. The British government set May 15, 1948 as the date of its withdrawal from Palestine, and would not permit the United Nations to enter before then to work out the transition to independence.

Exactly one month after the assembly's action, Rabbi Silver discussed the Arabs' use of terror to intimidate the United Nations and sabotage partition. He also showed how the critics of partition, by charging that partition would serve Soviet designs, sought to capitalize on the mounting tide of anti-Communist sentiment. The Zionist leader called upon the United States to assist actively in the implementation of partition. Just as the government had responded to the needs of Greece and Turkey with the Truman Doctrine, so was it committed to do more than leave the Palestine issue in the lap of the United Nations.

The heart of the matter, as Jewish spokesmen had maintained even before the vote on partition, was enforcement. British responsibility and Arab goodwill were not forthcoming. If the United Nations and the United States were not prepared to back up the decision, the fate of partition would rest on the Arab-Jewish battlefield. Or, Arab resistance could lead the United Nations and the United States to rethink and even scrap the entire resolution.

The American vote for partition did not mean that the opposition had evaporated. During the winter of 1947–48 there was a strong resurgence of the influence of the anti-Jewish state elements. Arab pressures on Washington and on American oil companies increased, reinforcing the arguments of those who maintained that partition jeopardized the national interest. Spokesmen for the oil interests and the military testified along those lines before congressional committees. Secretary of Defense James Forrestal, a bitter anti-Zionist who labored futilely to depoliticize the Palestine question, ran a virtual crusade for reappraisal of the United Nations' decision. Vehement in his denunciation of the Zionists for their pressure tactics, of politicians for listening to them, and of partition for its harm to American needs, he feared that the United States might be swept into a unilateral action of enforcement, which would require at least a partial mobilization. Senator Arthur Vandenberg, Republican chairman of the Senate Foreign Relations Committee, said that he would not accept unilateral action, warning that it could lead to the eruption of violent anti-Semitism in the United States. In the State Department, Under-Secretary Lovett and other officials agreed with Forrestal. A paper prepared by the department's planning staff in January stated that partition was unworkable if force and unilateral American action were to be avoided. Were the United States to become engaged in a war with the Arabs, the Russians no doubt would be waiting on the side, ready to pounce. Lovett, who was critical of Truman's independent course on Palestine, which bypassed the State Department, believed that if the United States were not hemmed in by the United Nations (used by other nations as a "propaganda platform"), it could deal more effectively with the Arabs and Jews. Despite protests in the House and Senate against the embargo on arms, and the mail campaign on that issue directed by the Zionists to Truman, the government would not lift its restrictions. Truman, too, was growing tired of Zionist pressures. "One of our principal difficulties in getting the Palestine matter settled," he wrote a petitioner, "has been that there are so many people in this country who know more about how the situation should be handled than do those in authority." [14] Although he was anxious about the deteriorating situation in Palestine, he refused to discuss the matter or even to see Dr. Weizmann in February.

In February 1948 a new anti-Zionist group, the Committee for Justice and Peace in the Holy Land, was organized, with Virginia Gildersleeve, recently retired head of Barnard College, as its elected chairman. According to her, almost all Americans with any experience in the Middle East believed that the Zionist goal was antithetical to American interests, to world peace, and to basic common justice. Inhibited heretofore from speaking out by guilt generated by the Holocaust, political reasons, or fears of evoking charges of anti-Semitism, they (e.g., Kermit Roosevelt, Dr. Henry Sloane Coffin, Rabbi Morris Lazaron of the American Council for Judaism) could no longer stand by silently. A delegation from the committee saw Secretary of State Marshall and added their support to the movement for reconsidering partition.

The war in Palestine confirmed the argument that partition could not be effected peaceably. The opposition derived even greater strength from the intensification of the Cold War in 1947–48. Competition and suspicions generated by the adoption of the Marshall Plan and the creation of the Cominform, a hardening impasse with respect to Germany, and the fall of Czechoslovakia to the Soviets widened the rift between Russia and the West. At home, investigations of Communists were gathering momentum under the House Un-American Activities Committee; Truman's Loyalty Review Board was getting under way. In that atmosphere an alliance with Russia, even on partition, would be distasteful and suspect. Besides, since Russia favored partition, that plan was obviously to its advantage in the struggle against the United States. Given Soviet aggressiveness, it was all the more important to keep Palestine as a Western base and to insure the flow of oil for the success of the ERP and for American defense. Soviet policies also made the enforcement of partition undesirable in a multilateral operation: (1) If Russian troops went in, would they ever be willing to leave? (2) Why tie up American troops in the Middle East when the situation in Europe was growing increasingly explosive?

At the end of February Warren Austin, American representative to the United Nations, announced that the Security Council was not empowered to use troops to back up a political settlement. This was the answer to the Jewish Agency and the Zionist sympathizers, who had asked for an international force, and to the United Nations committee on implementing partition, which had requested armed assistance in the discharge of its responsibilities. Zionists and their supporters denounced the statement. Aware that the opposition was gaining ground in the move to secure a reversal of partition, they had again, in mid-February, launched a letter-writing campaign, staged rallies, and elicited expressions of support from government officials, organized labor, and veterans groups. Now they had the assistance of those who read the American statement as a blow to the United Nations. The American Association for the United Nations convened a meeting of sixty organizations which called for the imposition of nonmilitary sanctions against the Arabs for flouting the United Nations' decision. An Emergency Committee to Save the United Nations by Supporting the Palestine Resolution was organized to conduct a campaign to arouse the public. Rabbi Silver reminded the Security Council that enforcement was the test facing the United Nations.

Fearing a forthright reversal by the United Nations, Weizmann appealed to Truman. Eddie Jacobson was the intermediary, and he persuaded the president to receive the Zionist leader. On March 18 Truman assured Weizmann that he still supported partition. According to the president's *Memoirs,* the two men knew at the end of the interview where each stood.

The very next day Austin addressed the Security Council and called for an immediate truce in Palestine, an end to partition efforts, and the consideration of a trusteeship for Palestine. Coming on the heels of Truman's assurances, it was a particularly severe blow to the Zionists. The president too was caught off guard. He had not authorized the release although he had approved the trusteeship plan as a standby device when it had been drawn up. Publicly he went along, explaining a few days later: "The trusteeship does not prejudice the character of the final political settlement. It would establish the conditions of order which are essential to a peaceful solution." [15] For the sake of his personal prestige, and that of the United States and the United Nations, Truman was not ready to scrap partition. He informed Weizmann that the new American posture did not mean a reversal of long-range objectives. On the other hand, he was still not ready to implement partition with force, and events since November proved that it could not work out by itself. The situation in Palestine was deteriorating steadily, and like most officials Truman believed that continued warfare would result in the annihilation of the Yishuv. Therefore, he wanted a truce for ending the conflict, and he agreed to a temporary trusteeship to provide the respite for working out a peaceful solution.

A Senate memorandum and a report of Secretary Marshall's testimony before the Senate Foreign Relations Committee disclosed other factors recommending trusteeship. Primarily, it bypassed the use of Russian troops, which the implementation of partition would have involved. The plan called for control by the United Nations Trusteeship Council, on which the Soviet Union was not represented. Furthermore, unlike the case of partition (defined as a *political* settlement), the use of troops could be justified because the trustees would be responsible for the maintenance of peace.

Despite the explanations, the public reacted angrily to the new policy. The administration was sharply criticized for its vacillating posture and for not having anticipated the implications of partition. Nor did the public or congressional leaders grasp any distinction between the use of force for partition as opposed to trusteeship. The influential New York newspapers, the *Herald-Tribune* and the *Times,* doubted whether trusteeship held out any greater promise of agreement or stability.

Most critics went on to attack the betrayal of the United Nations and the "sellout" of Zionism. Munich, the symbol of the most shameful level of appeasement, was used to describe America's stand. The United States had capitulated to Arab violence; it was prepared to use force against the establishment of a Jewish state rather than force the Arabs to accept a United Nations decision. As for the United Nations, it was following the same course taken by the League of Nations in the Manchurian and Ethiopian episodes.

New York Democrats threatened to break with Truman in the upcoming elections. The Federal Council of the Churches of Christ asserted that the government, under the control of the military, was threatening world peace and the United Nations. Andrei Gromyko, Soviet deputy foreign minister, accused the United States of sacrificing partition and the United Nations to its oil and military interests. American Zionists vented their anger in rallies, picketing, and letters to Washington. Categorically rejecting trusteeship, Zionist leaders declared that the Yishuv would go ahead on its own if necessary. Weizmann summed it up in the following words to Truman: "The choice for our people, Mr. President, is between statehood and extermination." [16]

The administration did not expect its proposal to arouse such bitter condemnation. On the international scene the reversal lowered America's prestige with the smaller nations. Nor did the new plan succeed in patching up the country's differences with Britain. The United States was not prepared to commit itself unconditionally to the use of troops to back up trusteeship, and the scheme bogged down in the deliberations at the United Nations.

Simultaneously, American resolutions calling for an end to hostilities in Palestine were proving ineffectual. United States officials tried persuasion and threats to force Jewish Agency leaders to suspend their activities for launching a state on May 15. But the Yishuv would not be sidetracked by what it considered stalling devices. In fact, Weizmann said, the same American officials would respect the Jews more for carrying out their plans for independence and *not* heeding American advice.

During April the military situation brightened for the Jews. The Haganah, a militia-turned-army, succeeded in routing the Arab forces near Jerusalem and Haifa. The intensity of the fighting mounted, and reprisals were followed by counter-reprisals. As the Jews proceeded to establish control over an area roughly corresponding to that which partition had envisaged, large numbers of Palestinian Arabs evacuated towns and villages and fled to neighboring Arab lands.

Meantime, preparations were being made for launching the new state. All sorts of questions—from the constitution of the country to the issuance of postage stamps—were raised and discussed. Finally, on the afternoon of May 14, David Ben-Gurion, who would become Israel's first prime minister, stood before the provisional parliament assembled in Tel Aviv to read the declaration of independence. It was eminently fitting that a portrait of Herzl graced the hall. The declaration said in part: "By virtue of the natural and historic right of the Jewish People and the Resolution of the General Assembly of the United Nations, we hereby proclaim the establishment of the Jewish State in Palestine, to be called Medinat Yisrael." [17] The British high commissioner set sail from Palestine shortly before midnight. At twelve the mandate was officially terminated and the State of Israel came into being.

Minutes later the United States announced its recognition of the new state. That act, another seeming reversal by the government, caught the American delegation to the United Nations by surprise. This time Truman upstaged the "striped-pants boys" and the anti-Zionists of the State Department. In light of the changed military situation, he now believed that support of the new government, a fait accompli, could sooner lead to peace than further United Nations action, which could not be enforced. Had the original test of enforcing partition been met squarely, and Arab aggression thus been forestalled, the same results could have been achieved without damage to America's image as a world leader.

After more than two thousand years, independent Jewish life was renewed in Palestine. Jews and Christians, East and West, dreamers and workers, capitalists and socialists—many had worked to that end. And so, by their deaths, had the six million victims of nazism. But the survival of the state was not yet assured. For the next twenty-five years Israel was forced to work on several "miracles" simultaneously: to maintain its independence against hostile and more populous neighbors bent on its destruction; to make the desert bloom so that an area roughly the size of New Jersey could absorb yet more and more immigrants; to remember for its own sake as well as for the sake of world Jewry that it was Jewish as well as a state.

7

Cold War Politics

Israel's declaration of independence and de facto recognition by the United States did not reconcile the Arabs or insure the security of the new state. Nor could Israel rely upon the United Nations to protect the nation it had created. While the armies of the neighboring states invaded Israel and hostilities raged, the United Nations discussed truces and armistices, considered the plan submitted by mediator Count Bernadotte for reducing the territory of Israel, and appointed a Palestine Conciliation Committee to resolve the issues of the Arab-Israeli impasse. No peace settlement was concluded, but the victories of the Israeli army forced the Arab states of Egypt, Jordan, Lebanon, and Syria to sign armistice agreements (February–July 1949). Israel now held almost five thousand square kilometers more than the area assigned it, but its enemies refused to accept the boundaries or Israel's very existence. For the next twenty years the deadlock persisted, compounded by subsidiary issues which were dumped into the international lap: a Jerusalem divided between Jordan and Israel, the plight of the Arab refugees who had fled Israeli-occupied territory, raids and retaliatory strikes across the borders, denial to Israeli shipping of passage through the Suez Canal and the Straits of Tiran, economic boycotts. The United Nations proved largely ineffectual, for both sides cooperated with the international body only when it suited their respective purposes.

I

During Israel's first year, its friends in the United States looked to the American government for continued support to stabilize the new state. The lightning speed of American recognition and the courtesies extended to Dr. Weizmann, the president of the new state, who stayed at Blair House in May 1948 as Truman's guest, had been good signs. Israel

94

also received the expected pledges in the platforms of the major political parties and from their candidates. (The Republicans attacked the administration for having vacillated on Palestine. Henry Wallace's Progressives coupled generous promises of aid to Israel with an appeal to the Arab people "not to permit themselves to be used as tools in a war against Israel on behalf of British and American monopolies.") [1] But the State Department, still at variance with the president, hoped to placate the Arabs as well as the British by resisting pro-Israel commitments. The net results for that first year showed, however, a very favorable balance. The United States extended de jure recognition to Israel and appointed James G. McDonald, a longtime friend of Zionism, as its first ambassador. In addition the American government warmly supported Israel's application for membership in the United Nations and a credit of one hundred million dollars from the Export-Import Bank.

Since government support did not come forth automatically, Zionists felt justified in continuing their activities for generating public sympathy toward Israel. To that end they articulated the duty of American Jews to share responsibility for Israel's political and economic well-being. Henry Morgenthau, chairman of the United Jewish Appeal in 1948 and a non-Zionist, echoed these ideas: "To me, the most important Jewish issue before the Jews of America is the success of the State of Israel. Any element which would retard or defeat that success must have our unyielding opposition." [2] Until 1954 the American Zionist Council, successor to the AZEC and umbrella organization of the major Zionist parties, led the public-relations drive. Then, operations aimed at influencing government policy were taken over by a duly registered lobbying agency, the American Zionist Committee for Public Affairs (AZCPA). In order to enlist the cooperation of non-Zionists and coordinate efforts, Dr. Nahum Goldmann, chairman of the New York office of the Jewish Agency, set up the Presidents' Conference in 1954 through which the heads of sixteen Zionist and non-Zionist national organizations considered aspects of American policy in the Middle East. Frequently, different agencies, acting in their individual capacities, supplemented the Zionist campaigns with activities of their own.

The goals of the public-relations work on behalf of Israel were to secure public and government assistance which would insure the future of the independent Jewish state and commit the United States to its preservation. Zionists and non-Zionists united on that platform, for support of Israel, now an established fact, was no longer a divisive issue within the Jewish community. [3] They operated both privately and publicly. Delegations approached the president and State Department, and individuals testified before congressional committees. Statements of support from congressmen and opinion-molders were solicited and publicized. The Zionist organizations distributed their own publications and utilized other mass media to develop a pro-Israel climate of opinion. The American Zionist Council sponsored lectures and guest appearances by Israeli visitors. When the ZOA was accredited to the United Nations as a non-governmental organization, it used informal conferences with diplomats and other nongovernmental organizations to disseminate its views. On certain occasions communities held mass rallies or undertook activities suggested by the AZCPA. As in the prestate period, Zionists cultivated their alliances with Christian and labor groups. Through the American Christian Palestine Committee and its own commission on interreligious affairs, the American Zionist Council worked with the Christian clergy, religious press, and interdenominational groups for an understanding of Middle Eastern issues. Zionists also sought commitments from political candidates, and they were careful to emphasize the bipartisan nature of their cause. (Democratic Senator Herbert Lehman of New York and Republican Senator Robert Taft of Ohio, who differed on most issues of domestic policy, found common ground in their support of Israel.)

The Jewish leaders who privately defended the needs of Israel to government officials were more than petitioners. They served as mediators, conciliators, and "honest brokers." With access to representatives of the two countries—a fact known and utilized by both sides—they labored behind the scenes to adjust differences and reconcile viewpoints. They explained United States policies and relayed off-the-record advice to Israeli representatives. They added their own views and criticisms, for theirs was no blanket endorsement of the Israeli line. At the same time they helped interpret to American leaders Israel's position on various issues and American Jewish concern with those issues. They saw no cause to explain their interest in Israel, for they operated on the assumption that a pluralistic society sanctioned differing group opinions. As intercessors for Israel they were most successful in their efforts to secure American economic aid. Their influence on Israel's policy was more discernible, since Israel was the dependent nation with respect to both the American government and the American Jewish community. For example, American Jewish pressure contributed to the stifling of pro-Soviet impulses on the part of the new state. In one case, a public campaign against Egypt, Zionist activity may have worsened Israeli-Egyptian relations. But over the years Israel appreciated the cooperation more than it resented the impingements on its policymaking.

In their pleas for Israel, American Jews benefited from the positive emotional response which Israel aroused in Americans. Non-Jews sympathized with the plucky David who had vanquished the Arab Goliath. Also, they could hear echoes of their country's past in Israel's pioneering spirit and of their religious heritage in the restoration of Zion. But the primary justification derived from the rhetoric which accompanied containment of Soviet ambitions, the leitmotif of American foreign policy in the postwar era. If the ideological thrust was to shore up the strength of the democracies against the threat of Soviet totalitarianism, Israel, the only reliable democracy in the Middle East, merited American support. "The free peoples of the world look to us," the president charged the nation in what became known as the Truman Doctrine, "for support in maintaining their freedoms." [4] In fact, as the outpost of Western democratic ideals, Israel was a natural asset to the United States. In 1950, by its unequivocal support of American action in Korea, Israel abandoned any hopes it might have entertained for a policy of neutralism in the Cold War. A year later Senators Douglas and Taft stated, when they introduced a bill for aid to Israel: "Israel is a bulwark in that area for world democracy." [5] Supporters of Israel also stressed its industrial potential, scientific progress, and proved military capacity. With American aid, they said, Israel could become a vital link in the democratic chain of defense. The National Security Council reasoned along similar lines in 1951: "It is in the interest of the United States that Israel remain free and independent, as well as friendly to the United States. . . . Curtailment of United States technical and economic assistance . . . would affect adversely United States security interests." [6]

To the government, however, containment in the Middle East did not mean an unqualified partnership with Israel. First and foremost, the United States sought to insure its military bases and strategic advantages as well as its access to the oil of the Middle East. The security of these interests depended on policies that would foster peace and stability within the region, harmonize Middle Eastern concerns with those of the United States, and thereby render impotent Russian imperialist designs. The rising tide of Arab nationalism and the eclipse of Britain as traditional stabilizer of the area complicated the task. So did the Arab-Israeli conflict.

As long as the United States tried to cultivate Arab goodwill for the attainment of its larger objectives, Israel's very existence, let alone the support it received from the United States, magnified the obstacles. The Arabs bitterly and consistently resented the United States' role in the establishment of the new state, and in Arab eyes Israel even became the symbol of Western imperialism. Since the Arabs refused to negotiate with Israel, peace and stability, the prerequisites for successful containment, became more elusive. In 1950 the United States, Britain, and France drew up the Tripartite Declaration, which sought to freeze the Middle Eastern situation with respect to boundaries and balance of arms. The arms race was slowed down for a while, but still no permanent settlement was reached. The declaration hinted at a regional defense plan, a tactic which the United States increasingly favored after the fall of Czechoslovakia and the outbreak of the Korean War, when it emphasized the military aspect of containment. American Zionists countered that a viable union against Soviet aggression could be built only after peace between Arab and Jew, and Arab and Arab, had been reached. Indeed, the Western proposal for a Middle East Command (1951–52) could not materialize, since the Arab nations still considered themselves at war with Israel and charged the United States with favoring their enemy.

II

The Republicans promised a "new look" in foreign policy in their campaign of 1952, but Secretary of State John Foster Dulles, who determined policy during the Eisenhower administration, adhered basically to the guidelines which had been set: support of the United Nations, containment, regional alliances. Since the regional-defense concept, patterned on NATO and SEATO, failed in the Middle East, Dulles tried a new tack. He approached the countries individually, beginning with those of the "northern tier" (Turkey, Iran, Pakistan). If they were allied in defense agreements, it was hoped that the southern Arab states would be influenced to join. In this way Dulles tried to separate the Arab-Israeli issue from the needs of containment. By the end of 1955 Turkey, Pakistan, Iraq, Iran, and Britain were joined together under the Baghdad Pact.

What disturbed Israel and its supporters in the United States was the State Department's determination to woo the Arabs even, as it appeared, at the expense of Israel's security. When the United States gave military and economic assistance to Iraq to sweeten its participation in a pro-West alliance, Israel feared that the arms would be used against it. Israel did not share Dulles's confidence that Arab states joined to the West could be prevented from renewing aggression. Its own pleas for participating in a Western defense alliance were turned down. Although American Jews and their supporters in and out of Congress criticized the administration for trafficking with undemocratic countries and shipping arms to the Arabs—a program, they charged, that was detrimental to *American* interests—their requests for arms to Israel and for a security pact went unheeded.

At the beginning of 1953 the Soviet Union broke off relations with Israel. That act, the culmination of a wave of intense anti-Semitism within Russia during the last years of Stalin's rule, sharpened Israel's feeling of isolation. Zionists reasoned that the Soviet action would encourage Arab aggressiveness, and their appeals for American support became more desperate. The American and Israeli descendants of those who had escaped the persecution of the tsar were threatened now by his Communist successors.

Zionist apprehensions that Dulles's announced policy of equal and impartial friendship toward Arab and Israeli would mean anti-Israel moves were proved correct. The United States cut off economic aid to Israel until it halted work on a hydroelectric project on the Jordan; the United States actively aided in the passage of a United Nations resolution censuring Israel for a raid into Jordan; the United States refused to move its embassy to Jerusalem when Israel located its foreign ministry there. On the other hand, the United States had no effective response to Egypt's blockade of the Suez Canal to Israeli shipping or to the Arab economic boycott of Israel. In view of America's studied cultivation of the new regime in Egypt after 1952, the Zionist press bitterly concluded that America was succumbing to Arab blackmail.

American Jews were also troubled by the sentiments that accompanied the government's announced impartiality. Assistant Secretary of State Henry Byroade advised in a public address that Israel see its future as a Middle Eastern state rather than "as a headquarters . . . of peoples of a particular religious faith who must have special rights within and obligations to the Israeli state." [7] True, the relationship between Israel and diaspora Jewry was a thorny problem to American Jews, but for a government official to presume to resolve that issue or to suggest how American Jews should behave was out of place. Byroade also announced that despite pressure groups, the State Department would be neither pro-Arab nor pro-Israel but only pro-American. The implication, according to a Zionist newspaper, was that pro-Israel could not be pro-American at the same time. Dulles's attitude, too, posed seeming contradictions. How could a man who read moral precepts into the Cold War refuse to distinguish between the rectitude of the Arab and Israeli causes, when the former, with no regard for democratic principles, was predicated on the extermination of a legally constituted sovereign nation?

A turning point in the Middle Eastern situation came in September 1955 when Egypt concluded an arms deal with the Soviets. Western control of the supply of armaments to the region, on which the 1950 Tripartite

Declaration hung, was over. Allying itself with Arab nationalism, Russia also showed that it did not need to resort to overt aggression for successful penetration of an area. Logic might have dictated that the United States respond with an arms shipment to Israel, and the latter's supporters expected as much. The Socialist Yiddish newspaper, the *Forward,* editorialized:

> The existence of the Jewish state is threatened. . . . We must assume that if the Communists have gotten a toehold in Egypt, they will aim at controlling the whole of the Middle East. . . . The democratic countries paid dearly for their betrayal of Czechoslovakia at Munich. . . . If the democracies want to safeguard the Middle East, they must act at once to adopt a strong and positive attitude with regard to Israel.[8]

The United States continued to appease Egypt's Nasser. It was forced, however, to withdraw an offer of financial help for Egypt's Aswan Dam project, since the pro-West Middle Eastern states resented the special treatment which Egypt, although hostile and often offensive, received. When Nasser proceeded to seize the Suez Canal, and simultaneously threatened the annihilation of Israel, Dulles would still not admit that Egypt's strong man posed a danger to the West or to Israel. He met with the president of the American Jewish Committee, who again recommended that the United States reaffirm its commitment to Israel and provide it with defensive weapons. The secretary was unmoved; even if Nasser bombed Israel, defensive weapons would be useless. No wonder that the ZOA, fully comprehending Israel's sense of isolation, published a chronicle of State Department policy from 1953 to July 1956 under the title *Calendar of Calamity.*

In October 1956, stirred up by Egypt's threats, inter-Arab military alliances, and the stepped-up commando raids into its territory, Israel invaded the Sinai Peninsula. England and France, which had their own scores to settle with Nasser and were in collusion with Israel, followed with an independent military strike against Egypt. With the United States in the lead, the United Nations quickly adopted resolutions ordering an end to hostilities and the withdrawal of foreign troops from Egypt. The diplomatic lineup had suddenly been turned upside down, for the United States found itself in league with the Soviet Union, then busily crushing a revolt in Hungary, in opposition to America's closest friends. Whether the Eisenhower administration was impelled to act as it did in an effort to stave off a major war, or to protect its image with the Arab nations, or to compel obedience to international law by abjuring the use of force, it significantly altered the course of events. Nasser's prestige was raised, France and England were ousted from the Middle East, and the United States was forced to assume unilateral responsibility for the protection of Western interests in the region.

Public opinion generally followed the administration in decrying the resort to force on the part of England, France, and Israel. Arab diplomats and student groups in the United States, and the pro-Arab American Friends of the Middle East, led in the condemnation of Israel's "aggression." Americans feared Soviet intervention and the outbreak of a world war. However, opinion polls and press comments still revealed a greater sympathy with Israel than with Egypt.

American Jews, too, were generally upset by Israel's strike. Zionist and other Jewish leaders attempted to set the Sinai invasion against its historical background, explaining why Israel was driven to use force. Presidents of sixteen major Jewish organizations issued a statement which combined an indictment of Egypt for its anti-Israel and anti-United Nations actions with the assertion that Israel represented the free world against "Nasserism backed by Communism." [9] ZOA president Neumann stated in a radio address that while the West followed appeasement, Israel alone stood up to the threat of Nasser and communism. In their public-relations campaign Zionists also drew parallels between Israel's response to the fedayeen (commando) raids and American action in 1916 against Mexican border raids. Warning against a return to the status quo ante, many Jews asked that the United States take the lead in bringing about direct peace talks between Arabs and Jews.

The administration's anti-Israel course of action was not deterred by such pressure or by the presidential election, which came a few days after the Sinai invasion. Democrats blamed the government's inept Middle Eastern policy for contributing to the hostilities, and Eisenhower's friends, according to the account of a *New York Times* reporter, warned that the president would lose New York. Nevertheless, Eisenhower refused to compromise his policies for the sake of politics. It turned out that he cracked all the traditionally Democratic religious and ethnic blocs except the Jewish; he carried New York and was reelected by a large plurality. The outcome showed that the power of the Jewish vote, at least on the immediate Israel crisis, had been overrated. That in turn reduced Jewish leverage with the administration still further.

Jewish differences with the government over the treatment of Israel did not emerge as a major worry. The decline of organized anti-Semitism and the growing acceptance of a pluralistic society had made the American

Jewish community more secure. Jews worried more about the fate of Israel and Nasser's moves against the Egyptian Jewish community than they did about incurring ill will on the American scene. They increased their aid to Israel through UJA contributions and the purchase of Israel bonds; they took personal pride in Israel's military victory. And, as one magazine writer put it, when Israel offered to exchange fifty-eight hundred captured Egyptians for four Israelis, all Jews carried their heads a bit higher.

In the main, public-opinion polls vindicated the Jewish response. Americans disassociated their fellow Jews from the Middle Eastern conflict. Of those who connected American Jews with the trouble, barely one-half thought they deserved to be blamed. But some responses did suggest that American Jews might be regarded unfavorably should more severe crises erupt in the future.

When Israel refused to comply with a United Nations resolution ordering its withdrawal from the Gaza Strip and Sharm el Sheikh, the two areas which Israel regarded as perennial trouble spots, Dulles and Eisenhower threatened the imposition of international sanctions. The United States had already cut off aid to Israel, causing a severe jolt to that country's economy. On the question of sanctions American Jewish opposition was reinforced by public sentiment. The Democrats in the Senate, led by Lyndon Johnson, and a group of Republicans under the leadership of William Knowland attacked the double standard which condoned sanctions against Israel but refrained from punishing Russia for military intervention in Hungary. Knowland even threatened to resign his seat on the American delegation to the United Nations. The administration answered that it expected more from the people of Israel, who were "imbued with a religious faith and a sense of moral values," [10] than from the Russians. That statement may have underscored the basic heritage shared by the United States and Israel, but it did not allay Jewish fears about military security. When Dulles arranged a meeting with eight prominent American Jews in an attempt to have them pressure Israel, he elicited only their anger and the bitterness of the Jewish community. Several newspapers attacked the secretary for intimidating the American Jews and for implying by the very invitation that they owed some sort of allegiance to Israel. Since none of the eight was known as a Zionist, the president of the ZOA called Dulles's act "a crude attempt to drive a wedge between American Jews." [11] The Zionists had expressed their own opposition to sanctions in a major rally held at Madison Square Garden.

Dulles was caught in a dilemma. To put through the pending Eisenhower Doctrine and make it effective, he needed congressional votes and Arab cooperation. The former could be lost if he punished Israel, the latter if he took Israel's side. The impasse was resolved when the United States delayed action on sanctions and Israel withdrew from the territory in question, banking on American assurance of free passage through the Gulf of Aqaba and on United Nations surveillance over the disputed areas.

III

The Sinai episode did not break the Arab-Israeli impasse. The two sides moved no closer on the issues of fixed boundaries, Arab refugees, and shipping through the Suez Canal. A permanent peace was as remote as ever. Despite Nasser's military defeat at the hands of the Israelis, the humiliation of the British and the French raised his prestige in the Arab world. Egypt's ruler set out to rearm his country with Russian aid and to establish Egypt's hegemony over the Arabs. The Soviet Union had not been deterred by the poor showing of its protégé. Russia was in the Middle East to stay, determined to curry favor with the Arabs irrespective of their form of government. On every level—arms supply, economic and technical assistance, support in the United Nations—the USSR forged ties with the Arabs and became a major competitor of the United States.

Arab esteem for the United States because of its stand against England, France, and Israel was short-lived. The United States now attempted to stem the tide of communism and Nasserism with the Eisenhower Doctrine of 1957. That policy pledged economic and military aid, and the use of American forces, to countries requesting it, against aggression on the part of other nations controlled by "international communism." Arab nationalists viewed the doctrine suspiciously, charging that it was a tool of Western imperialism to divide the Arab people. In the ensuing crises which erupted in Syria, Lebanon, and Iraq, the use of the doctrine failed to insure governments friendly to the United States. By the end of 1958 only Jordan was in the Western camp. America's plan for a regional pro-West alliance collapsed, and even the Baghdad Pact fell apart when Iraq withdrew.

Confronted by an independent Arab nationalism, disunity within and among the Arab states, and entrenched Soviet influence, the United States was forced to take the defensive. The most that it could do was to protect its remaining positions. The fact that Russia soon encountered obstacles to its own designs for increased control redounded to America's benefit. In a better position then to compete for Arab goodwill, the government, in the last years of the Eisenhower administration and the first

of Kennedy's, tried to effect a rapprochement with Egypt. With economic aid and the acceptance of independent Arab neutralism, the United
States was able for a few years to provide a counterpoise to Soviet influence. America's aims were more modest than they had been in Dulles's
days. It was content now to keep the Arabs neutral and not too greatly
dependent on the Soviets, preserving a stalemate with the USSR. Since
a nuclear standoff between the superpowers had emerged, the threat of
a major conflagration in the area was reduced.

The Arab-Israeli struggle could not be ignored while the United States
strove to construct a viable Middle Eastern policy. Israel remained the
one issue able to command Arab unity and the unresolved conflict kept
alive the possibility of a new eruption which could involve the superpowers. The presence of United Nations forces reduced the border raids
between Egypt and Israel, but sporadic forays and counterblows continued
along Israel's other borders.

Fortunately for the beleaguered state, greater accordance with the
United States developed when the echoes of Sinai died down. As long as
the United States was determined to resist Soviet advances, and insofar
as the Soviets abetted Arab designs against Israel, the interests of the
United States and Israel coincided. Israel still feared American military
aid to the Arabs, which could be diverted for use against the Jewish state.
But if the United States kept the balance among Israel's neighbors, preserved the status quo, and refrained from organizing the Arabs into
regional, and potentially anti-Israel, alliances, Israel had no cause to fear
American policies as threats to its national integrity. Furthermore, after
the Sinai-Suez episodes, the compatibility of interests between the two governments was strengthened by closer consultations on matters affecting
Israel's security. (Highlighting those consultations were Prime Minister
Ben-Gurion's private conversations with Eisenhower in 1960 and with
Kennedy in 1961.)

America's friendship with Egypt cooled off after the latter's involvement in the Yemen War of 1962–63. That war also reacted upon the
Arab-Israeli situation, for in response to Egypt's accelerated arms program
the United States agreed to sell weapons to Israel. Senators Jacob Javits
and Kenneth Keating of New York also took up Israel's long-standing
request for a defense pact with the United States. Members of Congress
who favored bolstering Israel's position and who resented support of
Nasser—which did not inhibit him from insulting the United States—
forced the end of rapprochement. Aid to Egypt was terminated in 1965,

reflecting congressional doubts about the efficacy of appeasement in winning political influence.

Both Kennedy and Johnson pledged American support for the territorial integrity of all Middle Eastern nations. The government continued to deplore the arms race, but by the mid-sixties the United States had become a direct major supplier of arms to the pro-West states. Whether it would be able to halt the military escalation and restrain the different countries before hostilities broke out—particularly in light of its increased preoccupation with Vietnam and domestic problems of racial strife and poverty—had yet to be proved.

IV

The Sinai campaign did not change the major thrust of the pro-Israel campaign among American Jews. Fear for Israel's security still dominated their thinking and colored their approach to questions of United States military aid to the Arab states, the Arab blockade of Israeli shipping, refugees, and the Middle East arms race. As long as the Arabs refused to negotiate a peace settlement and remained officially committed to the destruction of the Jewish state, every indication of softness on the part of the United Nations and the United States was a potential weapon to be used against Israel. In the decade after Sinai, friends of Israel hammered away at Arab intransigence and at the disinclination of the United Nations and the United States to carry out their promises to initiate direct peace negotiations and to insure free passage through the Suez. The immediate events leading up to Sinai had taught that periodic verbal pledges for the independence and security of Israel had neither prevented its isolation from the world community in time of crisis nor inhibited its neighbors from aggression.

American Jews learned another lesson from Sinai: an open rupture between their government and Israel was detrimental to Israel and potentially harmful to the interests of the American Jewish community. That consideration did not tone down their pro-Israel efforts but reinforced their aim to have the policies of both governments coincide. One approach was to show Israel's cooperative stance—for example, its approval of the Eisenhower Doctrine, its willingness to work with its neighbors in an American-developed water-sharing plan for the Jordan. When Zionists came to advocate American aid and friendship to both Arabs and Israelis, they showed a more sophisticated awareness of the aims of American policy. Another theme was to demonstrate the anti-Western posture of the Arab leaders. Nasser in particular was singled out as a Russian collaborator and untrustworthy ally. The rhetoric of the Cold War had toned down, but American friendship with Egypt was labeled appeasement if not blackmail. Egypt's president provided ammunition for such charges when he attacked the United States not only for its ties to Israel but for its actions in Africa and Southeast Asia. American Jews protested the seating of Egypt for a term on the Security Council (on the grounds that it flaunted international obligations), and they demonstrated against a state visit by Nasser to the United States. Jewish pressure had no effect on the administration's rapprochement policy, but it sustained the growing public and congressional clamor for the imposition of conditions upon economic aid programs.

Since both the United States and Israel found stability in the status quo, American friends of Israel were on constant alert to insure the maintenance of a balance between Israel and the Arabs. Jewish efforts for continuing American economic assistance to Israel were usually successful. By the mid-sixties American aid to Israel totaled approximately $1 billion (compared to $3.5 billion to the Arabs)—thirty-eight percent in loans, thirty-two percent in grants, twenty-eight percent in the use of surplus foods, and about two percent in technical assistance. Three hundred and forty American technicians served in Israel under the Point 4 program. They taught agriculture, animal husbandry, mining, and road building, and simultaneously forged bonds of mutual respect with the Israelis. At the same time Israel sent 640 persons to train in the United States and other countries. Point 4 aid terminated in 1962 after eleven years, when Israel was no longer deemed an underdeveloped country.

When Zionists asked for *military* assistance, they did not mean grants but rather the opportunity to purchase equipment. Israel was not rewarded with arms when it approved the Eisenhower Doctrine, for Dulles decided that it was "quite substantially armed." [12] For a while Israel received aid from France, but in the mid-sixties, facing encirclement by the hostile Arab League and the threat of a new war, its pleas to the United States became more desperate. American Jews took up Israel's demand with the government, pointing to Egypt's arms buildup, its use of German scientists to develop a missile system, and West Germany's cancellation of an arms contract with Israel in the wake of Egyptian threats. Agreeing that the balance was in jeopardy, the United States sold Israel ground-to-air missiles and other military hardware.

Concern for Israel's security was paramount, but in the years of relative calm it dulled to a chronic worry. During that period American

Jewish organizations fought an issue that derived from the Arab-Israeli conflict but involved them personally—the Arab League boycott. Primarily aimed at the economic strangulation of Israel, it began in 1961 as a boycott of companies with branches in Israel or doing business in that country. Later its scope was broadened to include a blacklist of American firms in any way connected with Israeli firms or owned by or employing Jews. Foreign ships that carried Israeli products or materials for Israel's defense, or stopped at Israeli ports, were denied services in Arab ports. Banks that loaned money to Israel, and even films featuring Israeli or pro-Israel actors, were under the ban.

American businesses in general were the victims, but if they severed their connections with Israel or became too reluctant to hire Jews, the Jews were hurt more. Jewish defense organizations also argued that the boycott not only violated American principles, which refused to condone discrimination among American citizens by foreign nations, but that it broke municipal and state laws forbidding inquiries into the religion of employees. Furthermore, the Arab inquisition into the operations of American firms was conducted on American soil and with the help of the federal mail service.

American Jews were singled out in another aspect of the boycott: restrictions on entry into Arab states. Some states refused outright to grant visas to American Jews, and their airports did not permit Jews in transit to disembark when planes stopped for servicing. Most states denied visas to Americans who also held Israeli visas. Jewish servicemen and civilian laborers employed by the American government were banned by Saudi Arabia even from the United States' own air base at Dhahran.

Although the government periodically expressed its opposition to these practices, in actual fact it went along with them. The Air Force Manual of 1953 listed the restrictions on travel in its instructions to servicemen. The Department of Agriculture and the Commodity Credit Corporation agreed that American ships carrying commodities to Arab countries, which were sold under foreign aid programs and hence supported by American taxpayers, would not stop at Israeli ports. When, in 1959, the New York State Commission against Discrimination investigated a complaint that Aramco (Arabian American Oil Company) was inquiring unlawfully into the religion of prospective employees, the State Department took the view that the agency's findings could not alter the situation. The department argued that the right of nations to exclude undesirable aliens was a domestic affair; it also believed that resistance would intensify Arab pressure and further jeopardize business interests. In 1960 the Seafarers'

International Union and the International Longshoremen's Association, backed by the AFL-CIO, picketed an Egyptian ship in protest against the blacklisting of American vessels that stopped at Israeli ports. Pressure by the State Department and promises of renewed efforts to fight the boycott ended the picketing.

Congress showed greater annoyance with the boycott than the executive, and some members favored linking foreign aid to an antiboycott principle. However, congressional sentiments were expressed as policy statements and not as law, and they were not heeded by the administration. In 1965 Congress was ready to prohibit firms from furnishing the data that fed the boycott, but the administration succeeded in having the prohibition modified to a mere request to business firms.

The Jewish defense organizations—American Jewish Committee, American Jewish Congress, B'nai B'rith, Jewish Labor Committee—were sensitive to the implications of second-class citizenship which the government's stand foisted upon the Jewish community. Publicly they maintained that as long as the United States acquiesced to Arab discrimination, it was betraying its moral professions on behalf of equal rights at home and in the international community.

Just as Israel had its partisans among Jews and non-Jews, who presented its case to the American people, so did the Arabs. The latter mustered strong support in academic and religious circles, many of which were integrally tied to philanthropic and educational institutions in the Middle East. Their strongest arguments were built on the issues of the status of Jerusalem and the Arab refugees. Opposing Israel's claims to any part of the city, they demanded internationalization of Jerusalem; Israel and American Zionists were only willing to accept international control of the holy places. With respect to the refugees the Arab supporters, like the Arab states, favored repatriation of the former Palestinians. Israel's partisans, however, blamed the Arabs for stimulating the exodus of refugees and for using that issue for political purposes. Fearing the buildup of an active fifth column in Israel, they stood for resettlement of the refugees, with compensation from Israel, in the Arab lands.

The propaganda duel between Zionists and anti-Zionists reached beyond the Arab-Israeli dispute, for Arab spokesmen in the United States attacked Jews as well as Israelis. In 1965 the United Arab Republic embassy in Washington distributed an anti-Israel pamphlet, which made extensive use of the infamous *Protocols of the Elders of Zion* and other stock anti-Semitic charges to indict Jewry at large for crimes against Christian civilization. American Jews were singled out by the ambassador from Syria, who declared in a public speech: "The American Jew is not an American emotionally or even ultimately." [13] On visits to the United States King Hussein of Jordan advised American Jews "to make an agonizing reappraisal" of their attitude toward Israel,[14] and King Faisal of Saudi Arabia announced that American Jews who supported Israel were his country's enemies. Arthur Goldberg was personally attacked for his Zionist sympathies when he served as American ambassador to the United Nations. One Cairo newspaper called Goldberg's appointment eminently logical, since "Zionists are the ones who direct American policy." [15] American Jews publicly countered these insults, which took advantage of diplomatic courtesy and American hospitality. More significant, however, was the fact that the Arab charges reinforced the native anti-Semitic movements.[16]

The tasks of Jewish defense and philanthropic organizations increased with other side effects of the Arab-Israeli dispute. For example, the establishment of the Jewish state and the Sinai campaign led to widespread punitive measures and persecution by some Arab states in the Middle East and North Africa against their native Jewish communities. Behind the Iron Curtain, too, the equation Jew = Zionist (and by implication pro-West) fed the current of government-sponsored anti-Semitism. The multiple problems of physical relief, protection of legal rights, fighting for the right to emigrate, finding havens for refugees and transporting them there—fell primarily on the American Jewish community. Even the issues of reparations from West Germany to Israel and Israel's trial of Nazi executioner Adolf Eichmann, both touching upon Israel's right to represent the victims of the Holocaust and the surviving remnant, were matters on which the organizations labored to keep the Israeli and American governments in harmony.

V

Despite the lack of government response on many issues, American Jews kept reiterating their requests and grievances. The defense organizations tackled the problems of foreign Jews and Arab discrimination against Americans; Zionists concentrated more particularly on the public-relations campaign on behalf of Israel. From the mid-fifties on, the day-to-day public-relations drive was led by the American Israel Public Affairs Committee, successor to the AZCPA. Registered with Congress under the lobbying law and supported by individual contributions, it submitted policy statements to the president and State Department and to Congress. It circulated the *Near East Report* to government officials, and its Washington and New York offices functioned as information centers for the public. Nonpartisan with respect to American politics, it worked for the inclusion of pro-Israel planks in the platforms of the major parties.

As had been the case since 1944, pledges of support to Israel crossed party lines, and generally the national platforms were eminently satisfactory to Zionists. Indeed the latter enjoyed an edge over other groups that expressed their views to the platform committees. In 1964, for example, both the American Council for Judaism and the Citizens Committee on American Policy in the Middle East testified against support of Israel. The former were still obsessed by the bogey of Jewish nationalism and people-hood, which, they feared, might tarnish their Americanism. Repudiated by the major American Jewish religious bodies and even ignored by the White House, the council and its propaganda constituted Jewry's own contributions to the Arab cause. That year the council sought to capitalize on a letter written by Assistant Secretary of State Phillips Talbot, which stated that the concept of a Jewish people did not exist in international law. Talbot's statement in its context was noncontroversial, but the council distorted it to imply that the State Department was lecturing American Jews on the issue of dual allegiance. The Citizens Committee, a pro-Arab lobby, reminded the political parties of the dangers of appealing to a minority bloc in light of America's strategic, economic, and diplomatic needs. They asked for an impartial plank, but that impartiality included the Arab demand for repatriation of the refugees. At the Democratic platform hearings, with the help of testimony from Congressmen Celler, Farbstein, Multer, and Powers, the anti-Zionist groups were defeated. The Democratic party resolved to "work for the attainment of peace in the Near East as an urgent goal, using our best efforts to prevent a military unbalance, to encourage arms reductions and the use of national resources for internal development and to encourage the resettlement of Arab refugees in lands where there is room and opportunity for them." [17] The Republicans tried to ignore the Middle Eastern situation, not because of the conflicting testimony but because of the split over foreign policy between the Goldwater conservatives and the eastern, liberal Scranton-Rockefeller forces. Under liberal pressure a plank was finally inserted which promised to prevent an arms imbalance and reaffirmed the party's 1960 pledges.

Just as party platforms took note of Israel and its needs, so did the contenders for political office. Eisenhower's handling of the Sinai invasion had not hurt his 1956 campaign, but four years later neither

Nixon nor Kennedy would risk losing the support of any group of voters. Echoes of Sinai were still heard, and the Nixon team had to live down the stories that vice-presidential candidate Henry Cabot Lodge had been the champion of sanctions against Israel. Senator Lyndon Johnson, Kennedy's running mate, was recalled as the man who opposed sanctions, but Kennedy's own image among Jews needed sprucing up. His record on Israel was one of indifference, and he was still dogged by the stories of his father's sympathy with Hitler. Both Nixon and Kennedy pledged their commitments to the independence of Israel and their active interest in establishing a lasting peace. Kennedy spelled out his peace suggestions more fully, but largely ignored them in his years as president.

That Kennedy the president differed from Kennedy the candidate did not reflect mere political opportunism. The executive was bound to consider the complex totality; congressmen and candidates were not privy to the totality but were sensitive to their particular constituency or audience. They could use a specific issue to political advantage even when they knew that their stand was unlikely to influence the policymakers. A case in point arose in 1966 when President Johnson met with the national commander of the Jewish War Veterans. According to the *New York Times* report, Johnson asked why there was so much opposition on the part of Jews to involvement in Vietnam at the same time that they requested American support of Israel. He was still the Johnson who had followed Truman and opposed Eisenhower in his friendship for Israel, the Texas rancher who sympathized with Israel's experiments in agricultural productivity. But he was also Johnson the president, who saw outside threats to two small countries (Israel and Vietnam) and no difference in America's commitments to the independence of both.

Since the establishment of the State of Israel, the record of Congress had been generally and consistently pro-Israel regardless of the executive's approach. Touched off by statements and resolutions by supporters of Israel, debates in Congress often included the condemnation of Arab, but not Israeli, practices. But while the Zionists' public-relations campaign may have succeeded with Congress and even large segments of the public, the decisions were not theirs to make. The case of American-Israel relations reflects the concentration of the power to make foreign policy in executive hands and the concomitant impotence of Congress.

One unpleasant episode arose on the floor of the Senate, and it concerned American Jews rather than Israel. In 1960 Senators Douglas of Illinois and Keating of New York sponsored an amendment to the mutual security bill which would have denied aid to nations that used blockades and boycotts or restricted the use of international waterways by other nations. Aimed clearly at Egypt, the amendment was attacked by J. W. Fulbright, chairman of the Senate Foreign Relations Committee. He charged that the amendment's sponsors were acting on behalf of "a pressure group in the United States which seeks to inject the Arab-Israeli dispute into domestic politics." In words which Jewish leaders subsequently challenged, Fulbright added: "In recent years we have seen the rise of organizations dedicated apparently not to America, but to foreign states and groups. The conduct of a foreign policy for America has been seriously compromised by this development." [18] By 1960 American Jews were too secure, and a pluralistic society too widely accepted, for Fulbright's statement to cow them into silence. Dual loyalty, except for the American Council for Judaism, was a dead issue. Indeed, as long as Americans repudiated isolationism and honored their international commitments, it was unlikely that a pro-Israel policy on the part of Jews or Congress or political parties would give rise to sustained or widespread opposition.

8

Redefining the Ties

The jubilation with which American Jews greeted the birth of Israel ripened into a new kind of pride, which increasingly characterized their community after 1948. "Every head among them was higher, every back was straighter, every brow was prouder," Professor Sol Liptzin has written of the reaction to the creation of the state.[1] When the Israeli national theater group or soccer team toured the United States, American Jews reaped added satisfaction. Most important in feeding their pride were Israel's military victories over its enemies. Such exploits, some of which were developed in contemporary fiction, helped to substitute the image of fighting, courageous Maccabee for the traditional picture of cringing, cowardly Jew. For some the state created new problems of identity, which had to be resolved. But none could deny the new dimension of dignity it bestowed upon all Jews. Sociologist Marshall Sklare concluded that American Jews gained a measure of psychological freedom through the existence of Israel. The gala Salute to Israel parade each year, he pointed out, was an example of how American Jews had abandoned their century-old reluctance to appear in public as Jews.

Yet the fact that Israel was a foreign state demanded major re-orientation on the part of American Jews. Zionists and non-Zionists were quick to warn against American Jewish meddling in Israel's domestic affairs, but the relationship between Israel—its government and its people—and the American Jewish community had yet to be mapped out. It seemed ironic that despite the major role played by American Zionism in the establishment of the state, the product spawned should be an independent, and in some ways alien, entity. When American-born Judah Magnes, who settled in Palestine after World War I and became chancellor of the Hebrew University, visited the United States in June 1948 on behalf of a group favoring a binational state, he had to register with the Justice Department as a foreign agent. In addition, major structural patterns set in the new society—advanced socialization, Orthodox control over religious life—were strange to American tastes. On the Israeli side, the new sabra generation, which came to maturity in the postwar period, contributed to the cleavage between the two communities by its indifference to and impatience with diaspora Jewry.

A far knottier problem for organized Zionism arose with the creation of the Jewish state. Once the political goal had been achieved, was there still a need for a Zionist movement? Did Zionists differ from other Jews who also contributed to the support of Israel? How meaningful was it for American Jews to join Zionist organizations, which were patterned upon the political parties of a foreign state?[2] Israel's security needs perpetuated American Zionist activities and institutions, many in their prestate form, but the underlying issue could not be ignored.

I

Israelis recognized their dependence upon American Jewry for political and economic aid. But many, like Ben-Gurion, refused to distinguish between Zionist and non-Zionist aid and, in fact, played down the importance of Zionism for philanthropic tasks. In the first place, they sought the backing of the larger community, which promised greater material assets and the commitment of greater numbers. Secondly, a Zionist's contribution, even if made with greater loyalty and steadfastness, was intrinsically no different from the contributions of other friends of Israel. The real Zionists, the Israelis said, were the ones who planned on aliyah.

Concerned primarily with Israel's manpower needs, Ben-Gurion chided American Zionists for their failure to settle in Israel. At the World Zionist Congress in 1951, other Israeli delegates warned Western Jews "it can happen here" or that Jews no longer fulfilled a meaningful function in the diaspora.[3] While some American Zionist leaders agreed that their movement should contribute settlers to Israel, all affirmed that the new state still needed a strong Zionist base in the United States. Two years later, at a Zionist General Council meeting, the debate came to a head. It was touched off by a letter from Ben-Gurion questioning the meaning of "aliyah-less" Zionism. The Israelis seriously suggested that American Jewry send them five thousand settlers annually. The Americans, however, could not be persuaded that aliyah suited American needs or that there was something wrong about feeling rooted in the United States or believing that American Jews could sustain their separate cultural institutions. They continued to insist that Israel could not write off the importance of the diaspora. Rose Halprin, leader of Hadassah and member of the Jewish Agency executive, warned of the dangers: "As long as you look on America only as a potential something or other for Israel, you will not help us, and, if you do not help us, you will lose Jewish life in its strength and its numbers." [4] Hadassah had resolved even earlier: "The conception that no one is a Zionist who does not come to Eretz Yisrael [Israel] is false. There is a need for a Zionist movement not only for the sake of Israel, but also for the sake of Jewish life in the Diaspora." [5] A decade later Abram Sachar, president of Brandeis University, reiterated similar views when he denounced "Israel Firsters whose chauvinism and arrogance find nothing relevant or viable in any area outside of Israel." [6]

In light of the historical experience of the American Jewish community as well as the course of American Zionist thought, it was eminently consistent for American Zionists to reject aliyah as their ultimate goal. They never believed that the laws of Jewish destiny formulated by Herzl and Pinsker applied to them. They did not argue Zionist doctrine but merely sought exemption for themselves. Political Zionism was not crucial to the United States, where Jews never had to fight for emancipation, or face a tradition of political anti-Semitism, or pay for political rights with assimilation. America was not exile, with the latter's connotations of persecution and rootlessness. Therefore, if Zionism meant redemption from exile, it was tailored for others. Zionism as a personal commitment, a way of filling personal spiritual needs, never characterized the movement in the United States. In the pre-Herzl days, a return to Zion was the vision of a few romantics. Twentieth-century Zionism was primarily philanthropy or refugeeism and hence generally ineffective in attracting the intellectuals. Brandeis tried to impart an intellectual meaning to Zionism, but he couched it in terms drawn from the American rather than the Jewish experience. A weak echo of that same theme was heard shortly after the establishment of the state. "We American Zionists know that Zionism is good Americanism," editorialized the *New Palestine*. "We know that the new Jewish State will promote the American ideals of freedom, peace, and prosperity, because these concepts stem from the ancient Jewish concepts." [7] Some critics thought that American Zionism had failed to capitalize on the resurgence of Jewish identification during and immediately after the war, particularly on the part of Jewish servicemen. The latter were especially "ripe" for conversion, for many had experienced alienation in the army, or witnessed foreign Jewish communities, or seen the work of the death camps. Even then, however, American Zionists did not swerve from the belief that their destiny was different from that of the Jewish people at large.

A study of the attitudes of American Jewish adolescents toward Israel at the end of the 1950s revealed the same outlook. Over eleven hundred youngsters about sixteen years old, all of whom were members of the B'nai B'rith Youth Organization, participated in the study. Overwhelmingly from upper-middle-class homes, most had had some Jewish education. The vast majority responded positively to Israel and the need for its survival. They recognized that religious and ethnic ties bound American Jews to the Israelis. But less than one percent favored permanent settlement in Israel by American Jewish youth. More than ninety percent rejected the classical Zionist teachings of the inevitability of anti-Semitism in the diaspora and the inability of the diaspora Jew to lead a full Jewish life.

Some Zionists may have felt guilty about not answering the call of aliyah. Others doubtless were resentful. Unstintingly they had served the Yishuv in financial and political ways; 1946–48 was, in the words of one observer, the "Golden Age of American Zionism." [8] Despite their support, without which the state probably would not have been created, their loyalty as Zionists was now being questioned.

American Jews also disapproved of the negative evaluations of their future voiced publicly by Israelis. The American Jewish Committee, for example, showed particular concern about statements that American Jews must immigrate en masse to Israel and that Jewish survival was doomed in the United States. Such comments, the organization insisted, fell into the category of unwarranted interference. They only harmed the position of diaspora Jewry and furnished ammunition to the charges of dual allegiance. In 1950 an "entente" was worked out between Ben-Gurion and Jacob Blaustein of the committee in a joint statement on the relationship of Israel to Jews in the United States. Blaustein expressed the beliefs of the non-Zionists:

> To American Jews, America is home. There, exist their thriving roots; there, is the country which they have helped to build; and there, they share its fruits and its destiny. They believe in the future of a democratic society in the United States under which all citizens, irrespective of creed and race, can live on terms of equality. They further believe that, if democracy should fail in America, there would be no future for democracy anywhere in the world, and that the very existence of an independent State of Israel would be problematic.

Aware that impressive support could be lost if men like Blaustein were alienated, Ben-Gurion admitted that the concept of the "ingathering of exiles" did not apply to American Jews, nor were their internal affairs any concern of Israel. He said:

> The Jews of the United States, as a community and as individuals, have only one political attachment and that is to the United States of America. They owe no political allegiance to Israel. . . . The Government and the people of Israel fully respect the right and integrity of the Jewish communities in other countries to develop their own mode of life and their indigenous social, economic and cultural institutions in accordance with their own needs and aspirations. Any weakening of American Jewry, and disruption of its communal life, any lowering of its sense of security, any diminution of its status, is a definite loss to Jews everywhere and to Israel in particular.[9]

With respect to immigration he said that Israel would like to see American Jews come, but that aliyah remained their personal decision. In succeeding years Israeli officials overstepped the limits of the entente only occasionally, and reminders from the American Jewish Committee brought them back into line. The entente itself was reaffirmed by Ben-Gurion and by his successor, Levi Eshkol.

Zionist and non-Zionist accord on the aliyah issue testified to the rootedness of the Jewish community within American society. Members of an urban, middle-class group whose vast majority was now native-born, postwar Jewry fit very comfortably in an increasingly urban, middle-class America. Economically their progress had been more rapid than that of the population at large. The median income of the Jewish group was higher than that of most other groups, and the majority of the younger generation were businessmen and professionals. Their behavior patterns and value systems conformed to American norms. Middle-class Americans affiliated with churches; Jews, though not more observant than heretofore, joined synagogues in greater numbers. Proportionately more Jews received a college education than other Americans, but society's growing emphasis on educational opportunities brought Jewish and American values closer together on that issue. Like their non-Jewish countrymen, Jews were also registering an increase in broken homes, abandoned children, and delinquency. Among the reading public, Jews as writers and as fictional heroes were finding new acclaim and sympathy. In 1954, when American Jews marked the three-hundredth anniversary of their settlement on American shores, past and present combined to renew their faith in their future as Americans.

A major factor explaining Jewish confidence and optimism was the sharp decline in organized anti-Semitism. Bigotry was now un-American, the province of the "lunatic fringe," the problem of the bigot rather than his target. In principle, at least, the quota systems of universities and professional schools had been cracked. New managerial jobs in the corporate economy were, for the first time, opening up to Jews. The anti-Semitism that persisted was principally of the "polite" variety—exclusion from clubs, fraternities, and preparatory schools—and in this area, too, Jewish defense organizations were hammering away with creditable results. In 1964, at a conference of social scientists, several participants concluded that for all practical purposes American anti-Semitism was dead or at least breathing its last. The survival of the Jew qua Jew, no longer fostered by outside negative pressures, had become a matter of individual option.

After the heyday of the prestate period, Zionist membership dropped. In 1956 the ZOA reported a membership of 106,000, which represented a loss of close to 150,000 over 1948. In fund-raising for Israel, too, the peak was reached in 1948. Thereafter collections for the United Jewish Appeal declined while those for hospitals and community centers in the United States rose steadily.[10] Jews expanded their synagogues, established new clubs, and gave their children more of a Jewish education than before. At the same time, however, they grew more involved in domestic political causes, particularly nonsectarian community relations and civil rights. The Jewish penchant for progressive causes, which political scientists are wont to note, was directed outside the Jewish orbit.

American rabbis shared their congregants' feelings of rootedness within the United States. Stressing the cultural and educational needs of the community, some warned against siphoning off the required funds into overseas philanthropy. Moreover, on personal and professional grounds they showed less enchantment with the State of Israel than they had with the Zionist cause of the thirties and forties. Since political activity was now the province of Israeli officials, the Zionist movement no longer needed, or provided a podium for, men with the talents and aspirations of a Stephen S. Wise or an Abba Hillel Silver. Most American rabbis were either Conservative or Reform, and therefore they also resented Orthodoxy's control of religious life in Israel and its refusal to recognize non-Orthodox practices. Finally, with the growing importance of individual synagogues in suburban society, rabbis frowned upon cultural endeavors within the community, including Zionist activities, that bypassed their personal spheres of influence.

The fulfillment of political Zionism with the creation of the state may have left a void in organizational activities, but for many Jews it merely reinforced the new direction of the Jewish community. To the extent that the average postwar American Jew identified as a Jew it was through the synagogue. He differed from his non-Jewish neighbor in religious rather than cultural forms. Cultural pluralism, in its logical implications, had never really existed; subcultures at variance with the dominant pattern could not flourish in the United States. Jewish thinker Will Herberg elaborated the concept of the triple melting pot, a boiling down of ethnic differences to three categories—Protestant, Catholic, Jewish—which, he claimed, more fittingly characterized the American scene. Only under the rubric of church were cultural deviations acceptable. In that climate of opinion the appeal of organized Zionism and other forms of secular ethnic loyalty would weaken. The history of ethnic minorities in the United States is one of disappearance through assimilation. Jewish cultural expressions not preserved by the synagogues seemed likely to disappear too.

II

The slow trickle of aliyah from the United States in the years 1948–67 reflected both the well-being of the American Jewish community and Israel's inability to come up with sufficiently strong countermagnets. Only at the very beginning of the postwar period (1945–49) did Americans respond in sizable numbers, and then most came to do a job without plans of settling. Some manned the Aliyah Bet ships that ran the British blockade with human cargo from the refugee camps. There were non-Jews as well as members of halutz organizations, and Jews drawn by sympathy, money, or a search for adventure as well as Zionists. Other Americans, ex-GIs, joined the Haganah after coming to Palestine to study at the Hebrew University. In the fall of 1947 Haganah organized the Overseas Volunteers for recruiting the military specialists, pilots, aircraft mechanics, and radar technicians that the Yishuv desperately needed in preparation for its independence. Approximately eight hundred Americans, mostly veterans, volunteered.[11] Many paid their own way to Israel; some brought along their own guns; all of the Jews and most of the non-Jews received no pay. A survey conducted among them revealed that eighty-three percent were American-born, ninety percent knew no Hebrew, and ninety-five percent had been unaffiliated with any Zionist organization. They were concentrated in the air force and air transport units, where the language was English and the style American. They flew Israel's planes and trained its pilots; they also took the lead in forging Israel's artillery and antitank corps and in establishing its radar system.

Haganah's recruiting efforts, like the mammoth drive for matériel and funds between 1945 and 1948, were conducted outside the American Zionist framework. The results of both, incidentally, helped to erase the differences between Zionists and non-Zionists in Israeli eyes. Ideological commitment played a part only in the separate drives of the halutz organizations. In March 1948 the council of Habonim, a halutz group of the labor Zionists, issued an emergency draft call. "Recognizing that the Jewish people are at war, recognizing that our enemies are bent on the destruction of the achievements of the past fifty years of constructive Zionist effort, recognizing that in the last analysis our own strength will be the decisive factor," [12] the council set out to mobilize members over the age of eighteen and prepare them for immediate aliyah. Two hundred left for Israel within the next nine months. However, by shipping out so many so quickly the organization may have weakened its appeal to younger members and its *halutziut* training program in the United States.

Between forty and sixty Americans lost their lives in Israel's War of Independence. The most distinguished of them was Colonel David Marcus, a graduate of West Point, class of 1924. Born on New York's Lower East Side to Rumanian parents, Marcus also earned a law degree and worked in the district attorney's office and as correction commissioner of New York. During World War II he returned to active military duty and served as legal aide at the summit conferences of the Allies. The sight of the concentration camp at Dachau turned him to active Zionism. After the war he went to Palestine, where he joined the Haganah under the name of Mickey Stone. In command of the Jerusalem fighting sector, Marcus was influential in planning overall Israeli strategy and in reorganizing the Israeli forces according to the demands of modern warfare. He was also responsible for the secret road that permitted supplies to reach beleaguered Jerusalem. In June 1948 a sentry's bullet ended his life.

Because Israel assumed that the American volunteers would stay on after the war was over, little in the way of counseling service was done to encourage them. Three hundred and seventy Americans decided to remain, but some of them eventually returned to the United States. The obstacles they faced were serious—unfamiliarity with the language, the economic hardships of life in a new country, which were compounded by military exigencies, and some anti-American prejudice. Nor were the Americans like the East European immigrants of the pre–World War I period, who turned their backs on the Old World and channeled their crusading zeal into building an experimental socialist society. The Americans, characterized by a pragmatic outlook, held more traditional views on family structure and religion. Unlike the first pioneers they had more to give up in the way of material comfort, and they knew that if the going got too rough they could always go home.

Israel tried harder in the 1950s to attract and hold on to immigrants from the United States. Aside from the strength of increased numbers, Israel needed technically skilled workers. It looked to the West for a supply of people familiar with the democratic processes to offset the possibility that Israeli society might be levantinized as a result of the influx of thousands of refugees from the Muslim countries. The immigration of Americans who were exchanging material comfort for economic uncertainty would boost the morale of the Israelis. It might also enrich the Jewish spirit of the sabra generation. Accordingly, emissaries were sent abroad; inquiries were conducted into why immigrants did not come and whether conditions in Israel could be made more attractive. The Jewish Agency maintained offices for advising prospective settlers, and it established a special Anglo-Saxon section. (The Jew, excluded by the WASP establishment at home, had become an Anglo-Saxon in a Jewish country!) After 1950 specific categories of *olim* ("immigrants") other than halutzim were serviced, for despite the resolution of Zionist organizations in favor of *halutziut,* the pioneer movement did not flourish. The new categories included middle-class families with small amounts of capital to invest, young professionals, senior citizens on retirement, and returnees (i.e., those trying aliyah after prior failures). In 1950 a private organization, the Association of Americans and Canadians, was created to help integrate the arrivals from those countries.

The low point in aliyah came in the mid-fifties. Americans were still absorbing the shocks of the Cold War; many were lulled into passivity by Senator Joseph McCarthy's frenzied witchhunt. The World Zionist Congress, meeting in 1956, appeared to have made peace with the idea that only token numbers would immigrate. One reporter noted: "On the whole it seemed that the matter of *aliyah* from the United States was treated as a subject one does not speak of in polite company, like sex in Victorian England." [13]

The numbers picked up after 1957. Zionist organizations, which had backed a "halfway" aliyah program in the form of tourism, investments, and workshops and seminars in Israel, grew warmer in their approval of aliyah. Never their sole aim, and never a vision of mass emigration, aliyah became a cardinal principle. The ZOA, for example, encouraged cultural aliyah for students—programs which combined work and study. The organization also held conferences and discussions for those considering aliyah, principally middle-class investors. In 1960 it established an aliyah department, and it recorded proudly how it had helped two Jewish cowboys from Texas to relocate in Israel. According to the ZOA, aliyah could succeed only gradually and only if preceded by a program of education for the Jewish community. The American Zionist Youth Foundation, which worked intensively with youth throughout the country, and the American section of the Jewish Agency also encouraged participation in projects taking adolescents and young adults to Israel. In 1965 Sherut la-Am (literally, "service to the people") was launched. Patterned on the Peace Corps, it recruited volunteers between the ages of eighteen and thirty to serve in Israel for one year. The participants filled jobs on kibbutzim or catered to the educational and welfare needs of the new immigrants. Between 1965 and 1967, five hundred Americans had enrolled in the program.

In the first dozen years of Israel's existence, roughly sixty-six hundred Americans (*olim* and tourists) chose to settle in the new state. Although about twenty-eight percent returned, the total number was augmented by about twenty-five hundred who took up residence there but held on to their American citizenship. Until 1960 at least, prior Zionist affiliation did not characterize the majority of settlers. After 1960 the Jewish Agency showed greater satisfaction with the results of programming for both Zionist-affiliated and nonaffiliated youth. It recorded an overall increase in the annual immigration rate from the United States and Canada—from twelve hundred plus in 1961 to seventeen hundred plus in 1967—and a decline in the number of those who returned. By 1967 the estimate for Americans who had settled in Israel rose to fifteen thousand.

Journalists, men of letters, and social scientists have written widely on American aliyah, suggesting different reasons why individuals did or did not immigrate, or why they returned to the United States. Author Maurice Samuel, for example, denied that evidence of persecution (the Holocaust, suppression of Soviet Jewry) was an effective stimulus for Americans: "Persecution . . . does not generate Zionism. . . . It paralyzes the imagination and leaves room only for confession. . . . And because pity, pity, pity, has been the everlasting theme of propaganda for the Homeland, the paralyzing effect has extended into the field of affirmation." [14] One Israeli psychologist talked of the "post-Zionist assimilationist," [15] the individual who joined pro-Israel organizations, gave money, visited Israel, rejoiced in its military victories, displayed his Jewish associations proudly before his non-Jewish neighbors, but felt thoroughly rooted in the diaspora. Some analysts concluded that the creation of the state helped eliminate the frustrations of Jews, assuring them that they were no longer members of an uprooted, wandering people. But the knowledge that there was a Jewish state in existence, and that exile had become a matter of choice, was sufficient to strengthen their feeling of belonging in countries outside that state. In other words, Israel's gift of increased security to American Jews worked against Israel's own needs for aliyah.

III

If American Zionists would not agree that their sole function was to prepare Jews for aliyah, they had to find other tasks to justify their existence. Serious diplomatic maneuvering, like that of the immediate prestate years, was now performed by Israeli officials. Nor could the Zionists claim exclusive rights to public-relations work on Israel's behalf, for now non-Zionists shared fully in those activities. Fund-raising, too, encompassed far more than Zionist efforts. True, Zionist contributions were still impressive. Hadassah sent ten million dollars annually to Israel for medical programs; the Labor Zionists and Pioneer Women raised forty-five million dollars between 1948 and 1962 for welfare projects in Israel. Zionist groups encouraged tourism to Israel, an important conduit of American dollars, and the ZOA found ways to expand both private investments in Israel and the marketing of Israeli products in the United States. But the principal source of financial aid remained the United Jewish Appeal, which collected funds from the entire community and allocated them for various philanthropic purposes. A supplementary source was opened up in 1951 with the launching of the Israel Bond Drive. Like the United Jewish Appeal it aimed at building up the Israeli economy and absorbing the new immigrants then streaming into the state, and it depended for its success on the cooperation of non-Zionist investors. When Ben-Gurion met with a group of American leaders in September 1950 to broach the idea, he found a parallel for them between Israel's goal and the American experience: "The oppressed of the Old World fled [to America], but they brought a vision with them, as do our immigrants today—a vision of a new life in freedom. They did wonderful things, and so can we." [16] The bond sales far exceeded the estimates projected by American investment bankers, and as a result Israel was also able to obtain loans from the Bank of America.

Non-Zionists as well as Zionists made private investments in Israeli industry and building developments, and specific organizations in the United States were established to handle these enterprises. Separate groups independent of Zionist organizations supported single institutions in Israel—for example, the Hebrew University, the Weizmann Institute, the Haifa Technion. Established non-Zionist organizations also subsidized their own pet projects in Israel. The National Council of Jewish Women sponsored a department of education at the Hebrew University, and the Jewish Labor Committee endowed a chair at the Hebrew University in honor of Abraham Cahan, the foremost American Jewish journalist and socialist of the early twentieth century.

Fund-raising for Israel served American Jewish as well as Israeli needs: the donors fed their own pride and self-confidence as Jews. If their contributions were sufficiently large, they also received some form of recognition—a personal introduction to the prime minister, or even an invitation to lend advice on certain financial or economic problems. They could never aspire to that kind of reward through American philanthropies, for in America the management of cultural and civil causes (museums, libraries, orchestras) traditionally belonged to the old established families.

Non-Zionists as well as Zionists contributed to the erection of "cultural bridges" between Israelis and Americans, for they too sought to maintain a cultural consensus between the Jewish state and the diaspora. Numerous groups, Jewish and nonsectarian, sponsored magazines, symposia, and conferences to foster mutual understanding through an interchange of ideas. They arranged for exchange visits of lecturers and artists from both countries to help cement ties of friendship. The Hillel Foundation established branches at Israeli universities, and the three wings of American Judaism—Orthodoxy, Conservatism, Reform—founded American-style religious centers. The American Jewish Committee opened a branch office in Israel and published a magazine in Hebrew on the style of *Commentary*. Even non-Jewish institutions aided in forging cultural ties. Harvard Law School made its resources available to Israel's minister of justice for the purpose of developing a unified system of law in that country, and the Library of Congress sent gifts of books to Israeli libraries.

These developments, along with Israel's studied friendliness toward non-Zionists and its criticism of the Zionist position on aliyah, caused Zionist prestige to slip lower. As one commentator observed, American Zionists "began to feel the agony of the mother who has given her last child in marriage":[17] What was there left to live for? The Religious Zionists still had their original purpose of fostering Orthodox institutions in the

United States, and Hadassah and Pioneer Women had built their organizations on social-service programs. But the ZOA, which had concentrated on securing a political state, and the Labor Zionists, who had worked for the establishment of a socialist society, had outlived their goals. Yet it was difficult for entrenched groups to vote themselves out of existence, and all organizations thought about reorienting their sights.

Immediately after the birth of the Jewish state and continuing thereafter, Zionists debated changes in organizational structure which would clarify the relationship between affiliates of the World Zionist Organization and Israel. Such changes were also suggested in order to delineate more clearly the roles of the Zionist organizations in the diaspora, interorganizational cooperation, and relations with non-Zionists on behalf of Israel. Despite the strictures of Zionist leaders against interference in Israel's internal affairs, the organizational framework under which the American Zionist groups existed as counterparts of distinct political parties in Israel led to such meddling. For example, the ZOA in 1951 aligned itself with the General Zionist party; Religious Zionists in the United States echoed their parties' protests over Israel's nonreligious education program for new immigrants. Israel wanted clear-cut lines of division, which would prevent interference from the diaspora, while American advocates of structural changes searched for a reformulation of the Zionist mission.[18]

The future of the Zionist organizations became involved with the question of an overall American Jewish communal agency. The American Jewish Conference discontinued its operations at the beginning of 1949, but public clamor for the coordination of Jewish communal projects persisted. Daniel Frisch, president of the ZOA, suggested a representative body built on a network of local community councils. National organizations would take their places within that framework instead of holding on to an independent and separate existence. The ZOA for one, Frisch maintained, would willingly recognize the authority and accept the decisions of the national body. David Petegorsky, director of the American Jewish Congress, advocated a mass democratic organization of individual Jews and the total dissolution of Zionist organizations. He was particularly critical of the Zionist structure, which could not successfully fill Israel's economic or public-relations needs. Nor could it serve to integrate the cultural activities of American Jewry and Israel. With over ninety organizations in the United States concerned with some phase of Israel, the Zionist movement, Petegorsky charged, only served to fragmentize the Jewish community.

Ideas for the consolidation or reorganization of Zionist groups bogged down. Two American Zionist Assemblies were held, one in 1953 and one in 1960, at which the major organizations deliberated the need for new programs. But little was done to implement suggestions for structural reform or united action with non-Zionists.

IV

In one significant area Zionist leaders did agree. Most urged that their movement concentrate on the stimulation of Jewish cultural and educational activities in the United States. They believed that in addition to studying Jewish tradition, which would include a knowledge of Israel and Zionism, American Jews had to create and sustain their own cultural forms. Jewish expression was not the sole prerogative of Israel, nor was American Jewry merely the repository of Israeli culture.

American Zionists had assumed little responsibility in the past for fostering Jewish culture or identity. But the new role they outlined was real and timely. Assimilation was threatening to erode postwar American Jewry as effectively as the Holocaust had destroyed prewar European Jewry. American Jews committed to the perpetuation of their heritage grew increasingly concerned as intermarriage and "dropping out" took their toll of the community. Jewish agencies, which heretofore had stressed defense work and social action, recognized the need to embark on programs emphasizing Jewish identity. Zionist cultural activity could also provide a counterthrust on behalf of group survival. Nahum Goldmann, addressing the first American Zionist Assembly, underscored the problem:

> It may sound paradoxical, but it is true nevertheless, that Zionism will hereafter be judged by its efforts for Jewish survival outside of Israel maybe more than by its efforts on behalf of Israel. . . . No less than our obligation to see Israel through its difficult period is our obligation to defeat indifference, combat disintegration, for these dangers are more imminent today than in any previous period in our history.[19]

Dr. Mordecai Kaplan, philosopher and founder of Reconstructionism, saw Judaism as confronted by the same crisis that Zionism was facing. To meet the challenge of assimilation spawned by secular democratic society, he called for a "New Zionism," a Zionism that would be a movement for the spiritual and cultural revival of Judaism in the modern world. He reverted back to the early cultural Zionists when he said that the establishment of a state was only a partial step. "Without a Jewish people regenerated in spirit, no matter how successful the state that it would establish, and how large a population that state could muster, Zion will continue to be unredeemed." He deplored not only the waning of Zionist idealism in the United States but the growing estrangement between Israel and the diaspora and the process of dejudaization within Israel. Therefore, it was incumbent upon both Israel and the diaspora to work in concert for the reaffirmation of Jewish peoplehood and the fostering of a modern Jewish civilization. Their needs were interdependent. "Should Jewish civilization fail to be at home in Eretz Yisrael [Israel], it will disappear everywhere else. Should it disappear everywhere else, it is bound to give way to some new Levantine civilization in Eretz Yisrael." [20]

Kaplan directed his message to world Zionism, but in essence it was an American position. It built on the premises that American Jews were rooted in their surroundings, that it was unreal to expect them to educate their children for eventual aliyah, and, the European Zionist thinkers to the contrary notwithstanding, that the Jewish experience in America was qualitatively different from the mainstream of Jewish history.

Kaplan's ideas were studied by the ZOA, and echoes were heard in the organization's deliberations from 1958 on. A resolution passed at the 1960 convention marked a new reading of the Basel Program and a deliberate shift in emphasis to cultural work:

> The Basle Program, while envisaging the establishment of the Jewish State as the first goal of the Zionist Movement, calls for the regeneration of the Jewish people throughout the world as the long-range, all inclusive aim of Zionism. This can be attained only if Zionists everywhere . . . steadfastly pursue as their objective the regeneration and reconstruction of the Jewish community.[21]

Other organizations fell into line, and in 1961 the American Zionist Council, coordinating body of the major Zionist groups, referred for the first time to the fostering of a greater knowledge of Hebrew and Hebrew culture as a *primary* aim.

The Zionists knew that by cultivating American Jewish culture they would not be turning their backs on Israel. Israel touched upon the lives of American Jews in so many ways that the latter were not likely to create an Israel-less culture. American Jews listened to Israeli records and decorated their homes with Israeli art and artifacts. As tourists they swarmed to Israel each year. Hebrew camps with a pro-Israel orientation multiplied; schools and even synagogues adopted the Israeli form of pronouncing Hebrew. Fund-raising for Israel was often sponsored by the local synagogue or Jewish community, thus rooting the activity in the American matrix and reacting upon the donor's social status within the American Jewish community.

The shift of emphasis by Zionists to education is more challenging than it sounds. It requires retooling workers and adapting machinery that were long geared solely to fund-raising and political lobbying. Furthermore, it is far more difficult to elicit public support for the teaching of Hebrew and Jewish history than for the arming of soldiers or the rescue of North African children. And if, according to the triple-melting-pot theory, the synagogue continues to supplant secular institutions in importance, Zionist organizations will have fewer Jews to service directly and will have to find ways of implementing their programs through the synagogues. Whether they can rise to that challenge may ultimately determine the survival of the American Zionist organizations. The fate of the movement as a meaningful institution depends on its own resourcefulness even more than on the needs of, or stimuli from, Israel.

9

The Six-Day War

In the history of Zionism 1967 was a milestone year. It marked the seventieth anniversary of the launching of the Zionist movement, the fiftieth anniversary of the Balfour Declaration, and the third military victory of the Jewish state over its enemies. As had been the case throughout the twentieth century, the reaction of the American Jews to the events leading up to the Six-Day War and to the war itself was shaped largely by their position within society and by the reaction of the American government and the American public. In this way the episode pulls together the various threads we have sought to unravel. However, the 1967 crisis was different on several specific counts: the absence of any distinction between Zionist and non-Zionist, the strains that resulted between the Jewish community and certain other groups, and the intensity of the Jewish reaction, which was unusual for a highly acculturated minority. If these differences prove more than ephemeral, the year may well mark a watershed in American Jewish history.

I

Conditions since 1957 foreshadowed a new Arab-Israeli outbreak. The Suez episode resolved nothing of importance. True, Egyptian border raids were temporarily halted, and Israel received America's vague assurance of the right to navigate through the Gulf of Aqaba. But the basic antagonism persisted, aggravated in fact by the Suez eruption. With France and England routed from the region, Israel was even more dependent upon the United States. The intensification of Arab nationalism and of Third World neutralism sharpened the differences between Israel and its neighbors. Soviet and Arab propagandists frequently made use of Israel's short-

129

lived alliance in 1956 with England and France to denounce Western, and therefore Israeli, imperialism. Smarting under their military defeat at the hands of the Israelis, the Egyptians looked forward to their day of revenge.

In mid-May 1967, Egypt began a troop buildup in the Sinai Peninsula and compelled the removal of the United Nations forces from the Sinai border and the Gaza Strip. On May 22 Nasser announced the closing of the Gulf of Aqaba to Israeli shipping—a move which Israel had repeatedly warned would mean war. Nasser's actions were stimulated in part by Soviet and Syrian charges of Israeli military plans against Syria and by suspicions of American designs in the Middle East. Prompted by a desire to enhance his personal prestige and by the pressures of Egypt's economic needs, he no longer advised postponing the long promised showdown with Israel. By the last week in May Nasser was calling for a general war against Israel. Arab threats to exterminate the Jews were sounded along with anti-American diatribes. In Israel the scene for war was being set with the hurried departure of tourists, the evacuation of British and American nationals, and the arrival of Red Cross officials and news correspondents.

At first the United States refused to believe that Nasser was doing more than playacting. When the new American ambassador arrived in Cairo on May 21, he flatly denied to reporters that a crisis existed. Faced with growing public bitterness over the Vietnam War and the prospect of racial disturbances during the summer, the government was especially anxious to see that peace was preserved. A Middle Eastern war could conceivably lead to American involvement and to a direct collision with the Soviet Union.

Russia shared America's concern to avoid a superpower confrontation. The Soviets had poured military and economic aid into the Arab countries since 1955, but their moves to entrench themselves while confining American influence were limited by the development of a nuclear stalemate between the superpowers. Neither one could afford to risk a policy which might push the other over the brink. Although Russia incited Egypt to take the first step of mobilization in order to deter an alleged Israeli strike against Syria, it was apparently not consulted on the next moves. When the Soviets saw that developments were out of their hands, they would not promise military intervention. Despite verbal threats and a show of strength on the part of both, the superpowers agreed to remain on the sidelines. President Johnson later recalled that the "hot line" had been used twenty-seven times during the crisis.[1] But Russia and the United States both failed to restrain the governments concerned from resorting to open warfare.

Even if Soviet neutrality was assured, the United States still opposed a new Middle Eastern war because it could only jeopardize American interests. Since the Arabs identified the United States with Israel, an Israeli victory would further antagonize the Muslim world. On the other hand, in light of America's commitment to the independence and integrity of the Jewish state and its assurance of free passage through the Gulf of Aqaba, an Israeli defeat would show other pro-Western states that the United States did not honor its commitments. However, once Nasser made his moves, the United States could have restrained Israel only by taking the initiative on the free shipping issue and forcing the Egyptian ruler to back down.

For a few days it looked as if the American government would stand firm. Realizing that Israel interpreted the Egyptian blockade of the Gulf of Aqaba as an act of aggression, the government immediately asked Israel to defer action for two or three days. A note also went to Cairo calling for Egyptian restraint and not ruling out the possibility of the use of force against the blockade. President Johnson, in a nationwide television address, reaffirmed America's pledge to support the territorial integrity of all Middle Eastern nations. Deploring resort to war, he nonetheless condemned the blockade in strong words:

> The United States considers the gulf to be an international waterway and feels that a blockade of Israeli shipping is illegal and potentially disastrous to the cause of peace. The right of free innocent passage of the international waterway is a vital interest of the entire international community.

He also consulted with former President Eisenhower, who asserted that the country was bound by a "commitment of honor" to protect the right of free shipping. At the Security Council, where international action toward a peaceful solution was hamstrung by Russia, Ambassador Goldberg urged that Egypt forgo the blockade while the United Nations dealt with the underlying causes of the crisis. Over one hundred congressmen signed a statement, prepared by New York's Emanuel Celler, which called on the administration "to take whatever action may be necessary to resist aggression against Israel and to preserve the peace."[2]

There is no reason to doubt Johnson's sincerity on honoring America's commitment to Israel. But, as the president explained to Israel's foreign minister, Eban, he was not a free agent. Vietnam cast its pall over all deliberations; government officials and the public, while sympathetic to Israel, generally opposed unilateral American intervention. Senate majority leader

Mike Mansfield reflected the mood in the upper house when he said: "There should be no question of unilateral involvement in the Near East." [3] Eisenhower, his "commitment of honor" notwithstanding, also called the issue a matter for the United Nations.

Secretaries Rusk and McNamara drew up a memorandum for Johnson, in preparation for Eban's visit on May 26, which attempted a reconciliation between American pledges and the avoidance of unilateral measures. It proposed that the United States assume responsibility for ending the blockade by trying first for United Nations action. If that failed, the United States and other maritime powers could insist, in a joint declaration, on the right of free passage. Only as a last resort the United States might be compelled to use warships to escort vessels through the Straits of Tiran. At the meeting with Eban the president referred to the plan for collective action for breaking the blockade, and he asked Israel to hold off for another two weeks to permit the scheme to take effect.

According to one analysis, the Johnson-Eban meeting was crucial in weakening the American posture. During the meeting Eban recounted his government's fears of an imminent Egyptian attack. Administration officials dismissed the fears as groundless, but they inferred from Eban's remarks, and from Israel's acquiescence to the two-week delay and to the collective-action idea, that Israel was unprepared for war. Assuming that it would not fight, that it had no choice but to accept what the United States could do, the administration no longer felt the same pressure for initiating action or for considering a show of force.

The United States continued to caution the potential belligerents against aggression. But the possibility of effective action dimmed. The United Nations was hopelessly impotent. The Western powers were divided on the Middle East situation, and the plans for a flotilla to escort ships through the Gulf of Aqaba mustered little support among America's friends. In Washington, the Pentagon, the State Department, and members of Congress expressed their opposition to a collective force. At one point the State Department even considered a scheme permitting free shipping to all nations except Israel. Clearly the United States had no workable plan within the limits of conventional diplomacy to honor its commitments. And, by concentrating on the blockade rather than on the threat of a land war— which, in light of the Arab buildup on their borders, was now the major worry of the Israelis—the United States lost sight of the broader dimensions of the crisis.

Israel yielded to American pressures by marking time, but it was never convinced that America's commitments automatically guaranteed its safety. In April 1967 Prime Minister Eshkol had stated in an interview with *U.S. News and World Report* that if attacked, Israel would rely on its own army. American officials had reassured him, when he tried to purchase arms, that the Sixth Fleet was in the Mediterranean; but, Eshkol stated, "the Sixth Fleet might not be available fast enough for one reason or another, so Israel must be strong on its own." Even if American guardianship could be taken for granted, Israel rejected the notion of complete dependence. Remembering the disadvantages of the alignment with France and England in 1956, the Israelis preferred to chart their own course. In a press conference beamed to American and British television audiences, General Moshe Dayan said that he "wouldn't like American or British boys getting killed here in order to secure our safety." [4]

When Johnson pleaded for a time respite, the Israelis fretted, knowing full well the weakening of America's position and their own increasing isolation. Meantime, the Arabs showed no signs of relenting and were busy cementing new ties of solidarity. Convinced at last that it was pointless to wait for an American diplomatic solution, Israel decided to strike on June 5.

The lightning speed with which Israel routed its enemies obscured certain troubling questions. If the war had dragged on, or if victory had gone the other way, would the United States have done anything? What was the meaning, value, or need for an American commitment if, as the prewar developments indicated, American action would not go beyond futile diplomatic deliberations? The United States silently hoped that the Israelis would handle the situation themselves, but that hope needed no grounding in "commitments of honor." America's deeper interest may demand that a commitment, if in conflict with that interest, be ignored, but such contradictions point up weaknesses in a country's foreign policy.

President Johnson's reaction to the Egyptian blockade proved that the United States did not consider itself neutral during the crisis. Nevertheless, a State Department spokesman announced, upon the eruption of hostilities, that the government "is neutral in thought, word and deed." [5] When questions were raised whether the country was abandoning Israel, the White House hastily explained that neutral did not mean indifferent. Although some members of Congress insisted that Israel was an ally, even they would not suggest military intervention. Congress was always more sympathetic to Israel and more receptive to pro-Israel pressure than the executive, but whether it would have forced the administration's hand had Israel not emerged victorious so rapidly is a moot point.

Both the executive and Congress were relieved of responsibility, and

of the very need to come to a decision, by the Israeli armed forces. Once
the war ended, relief turned to admiration for Israel's military prowess. On
the floor of the House of Representatives, Congressman Wayne Hays of
Ohio archly suggested that the United States trade "about 400 F-111 planes
for that one-eyed general [Dayan], and send him to Vietnam." [6] Nor did
the United States press the matter of the *Liberty,* an American reconnais-
sance ship stationed off the Sinai Peninsula, which was crippled by an
Israeli attack causing the loss of thirty-four of its crew. Israel promptly
apologized for the tragic error and offered to pay reparations.

Israel's victory redounded to America's benefit insofar as Russia's
protégés, and hence Russia, were defeated. On the other hand, anti-Ameri-
canism in the Middle East increased. The Arabs charged, and actually believed, that America had provided air cover for Israel's army—thus
accounting for the latter's brilliant success. Some Arab governments severed
diplomatic relations with the United States and put an embargo on oil
shipments. But by the end of the year normal ties were restored with most.

Thanks to the brevity of the war American Jews were also let off the
hook. They never felt constrained to challenge public and government
sentiment by calling for American military intervention. United in support
of Israel, they found themselves in a happier position than in 1956. In the
more recent episode Israel did not strike a preemptive blow but was clearly
on the defensive. It showed its good faith by acceding to American requests to defer action, and, like the United States, would have preferred
peace. Not only was Israel the underdog before the war, a position traditionally evoking American public sympathy, but it was menaced by
America's arch-competitor working through the Arab states. President
Johnson's strong words on America's commitment also proved that the
United States considered the cause just, and that support for Israel was
good Americanism.

From the end of May until hostilities ended, American Jewish groups
—the distinction between Zionist and non-Zionist no longer applied—
called on the government to honor its pledges. In a full-page advertisement
in the *New York Times* the Jewish War Veterans, for example, asked for
help to Israel for the sake of the United States and civilization. A rally held
in Washington on June 8 drew thousands of Jews to the capital to petition
on behalf of the Jewish state. But events obviated the need to fill in specifics
on what type of aid they wanted, for news of the cease-fire on the Jordan-
Israel front turned the rally into a victory demonstration.

However, had the war continued, or turned out differently, American
Jews would have been faced with a serious problem. Would they have set

themselves apart from the majority antiinterventionist position and pressured specifically for military assistance? Would they have demanded that the government honor its commitments with more than verbal protestations? In 1956–57 they had tried only to counteract the imposition of sanctions against Israel, far different from asking for troops or planes. Their efforts had not swayed the Eisenhower administration, and there is no evidence that their opinion a decade later was any more influential in shaping government policy.

The hypothetical question of what they would have done can elicit different conjectures. The issue doubtless would have split the Jewish community. Some might have argued dual loyalty, or that an unyielding pro-Israel stance would alienate many non-Jewish supporters of Israel and even fan the dormant flames of American anti-Semitism. When the chips were down, they would have argued, American Jews would have to behave like other Americans even if it meant turning their backs on Israel. On the other hand, some would undoubtedly have stood firm in support of Israel. American Jews were more assertive in the sixties than they had been a decade earlier—a result due in large measure to society's tolerance of new tactics of protest introduced by the civil rights and antiwar movements.

As it turned out, however, the Jewish community did not have to choose sides. In retrospect it could even believe that government support of Israel, and government accord with American Jewish opinion, was stronger than in fact it had been.

II

To the extent that they showed an interest in the situation, Americans were lavish in their moral support of Israel. Sympathy for the young democracy, victim of Russian scheming and United Nations ineffectiveness, was expressed in opinion polls and in the press. Most Americans thought the Arabs to blame for starting the war and held that the Israelis were in the right. Admiration for Israel's military ability reinforced public approval. (For its own protection the United States should sign a mutual defense pact with Israel, quipped William Buckley.) [7] The majority backed Israel's conditions for a permanent peace settlement—free shipping through the Gulf of Aqaba and the Suez Canal, Arab recognition of Israel's sovereignty. However, the overwhelming number opposed direct involvement by the United States.

Right-wing American groups, traditionally cool to the socialistic Jewish state, also took a pro-Israel stand. They hailed the war as an example of a tough, anti-Communist policy and went on to criticize the United States for its own timidity vis-à-vis the Soviet Union. On the other hand, the leftist groups that followed the Soviet or Maoist lines condemned Israel and supported the Arabs. Identifying Israel and Jews with the American establishment, the New Left followed suit, despite a heavy representation of Jews in its ranks. Along with radical black nationalists they accused the "fascist," "militaristic," "racist" Jews of planning genocide and of perpetrating atrocities against the Arabs.[8] (The Third World nations in the United Nations did not follow so clear-cut a line.) At the National Conference for New Politics in September 1967 the blacks succeeded in forcing through a resolution condemning Zionist "aggression." Although some Jews broke with the radicals on the issue, the left-wingers held fast to their anti-Israel stand, which in some cases was a blatantly anti-Jewish stand.

Thus, the Six-Day War taught American Jews a lesson in politics. It helped destroy the belief, ingrained since Emancipation, that the left generally supported Jewish interests while the right was the source of anti-Semitism. The repercussions of that lesson could be significant in the development of political coalitions and interracial relationships within the United States.

The reaction of the public to the Middle East crisis, like that of the executive and Congress, was overshadowed by the specter of Vietnam and the resulting fear of a parallel type of involvement. The supporters of Johnson's Vietnam policy also picked up the issue as a weapon against their critics. How could one demand that the United States honor its commitment to Israel, they reasoned, and simultaneously condemn American intervention in Southeast Asia? Since some Jews who were prominent in the anti-Vietnam crusade were among those asking for a firm American response in the Middle East, an apparent case of double standards had arisen. A public statement on behalf of American support to Israel led presidential adviser John Roche to comment that it should have been signed "Doves for War." (It was in fact signed by both friends and critics of the Vietnam policy.) Some "doves" agreed, maintaining, like Arthur Schlesinger, that it was inconsistent to support unilateral intervention in one part of the world and oppose it in another. Others attempted to show the differences between the two situations or how American policy could be neither all "hawk" nor all "dove." Theodore Draper, for example, argued that the Vietnam "hawks" in the Pentagon were the arch "doves" with respect to Israel. Nevertheless, the oversimplified analogy between Vietnam and Israel was more persuasive. It resulted in divisions within the peace movement, and it caused some American Jews to conclude that the price for help to Israel was silence on Vietnam.

The group whose reactions most disappointed American Jews was the Christian churches. Since the end of World War II many Jewish and Christian leaders had invested great effort in interreligious activity. They sponsored dialogues, initiated joint action on social issues, and updated religious textbooks in order to cultivate mutual respect and understanding. Their most dramatic achievement came at Vatican Council II (1965), where the liberal Catholic prelates forced a revision of the charge of deicide against the Jews. In 1967, however, aside from some statements from individual clergymen, the official church establishments showed no sympathy when Israel was threatened with extermination. Years of dialogue and a partnership on issues like civil rights and poverty were overshadowed by long-established missionary programs and interests in the Middle East and by religious hostility to the concept of Jewish peoplehood. After Israel's victory, and specifically in the aftermath of its annexation of Jerusalem, both Protestants and Catholics were sharply critical of the Jewish state. Rabbis openly displayed their resentment over the churches' position, causing Christian spokesmen in turn to justify their views in angry terms. Henry Van Dusen, a former president of Union Theological Seminary, was most vehement when he publicly compared Israel's actions with Nazi Germany's:

All persons who seek to view the Middle Eastern problem with honesty and objectivity stand aghast at Israel's onslaught, the most violent, ruthless (and successful) aggression since Hitler's blitzkrieg across Western Europe in the summer of 1940, aiming not at victory but at annihilation . . . [10]

Although some Christians deplored the opposition or coolness of the religious bodies, Jews began to question the value of interfaith activities. If meaningful dialogue were to continue, it would have to come to grips with basic historic and theological differences between the faiths and not merely parade their superficial affinities.

With respect to public relations, the 1967 war showed that the task of Israel's supporters in the United States was openended. Arab propaganda was not the most significant problem, although it increased noticeably after the war. Nor was it crucial that Israel's popularity could only diminish after the peak it reached in June 1967. More important was the fact that the Israel issue, irrespective of its merits, was bound up with possible shifts in American foreign policy. And not since 1947, when the United States

embarked on its policy of containment, was the challenge to the principles
of internationalism so pervasive. If, in the wake of mass disaffection over
Vietnam, the United States consciously trimmed its internationalist sails, or
if the United States chose to unburden itself of all interests that threatened
a peaceful coexistence with the Soviet Union, its twenty-year-old commitment to Israel, for what it was worth, would be jeopardized. Similarly, the
question of Israel was woven into the broader area of intergroup politics
within the United States. If support for Israel were repudiated by the
establishment to appease its critics, or if anti-Israel or anti-Jewish groups
were ever in a position to demand that American Jews surrender their pro-
Israel posture, the Jewish state, as well as American Jewry, would be en-
dangered. To what extent American Jews can prevent such occurrences—
whether through alliances with the establishment, or through specific programs to foster cooperation with the churches or the blacks or disaffected
youth, or through concentrated attempts to strengthen the cohesiveness and
political bargaining power of the Jewish community—remains to be seen.

III

American Jewish support of Israel was not surprising, especially since
it coincided with government policy and general public opinion. What was
surprising was the intensity of the Jewish reaction. Unlike the immediate
prestate period or the 1956 Sinai invasion, the community closed ranks on
the issue and polls recorded near one-hundred-percent unanimity in support
of Israel's resort to arms. Anti-Vietnam sentiment in Jewish circles was
no stumbling block; and even the American Council for Judaism refrained
from public criticism until after the war. A Jewish Agency report asserted
that "never before has there been such an instantaneous manifestation of
dedication and concern for Israel and its people." [11]

Organizational wheels, Zionist and non-Zionist, ground more rapidly
after the onset of the crisis in May. Mobilizing their members in a major
public-relations drive, organizations sponsored rallies, disseminated information, petitioned government officials, and collected money. Specialized
agencies handled specific tasks. The Jewish Labor Committee, for example,
concentrated on eliciting support for Israel in general labor circles, and
strong pledges from AFL-CIO president George Meany were obtained. But,
different again from previous crises, American Jews did not wait for organizational directives. Even as they sat glued to radios and TVs or put in long-
distance calls to friends in Israel, they fretted over what they could do.
They organized meetings on the synagogue or neighborhood level, and

they donated food, blood, and medical supplies. Doctors and teachers volunteered to serve if Israel called upon them. On campuses special lectures and "teach-ins" were held as the traditionally alienated intellectuals stood up and were counted. The attendance at synagogue services soared, equaling the High Holy Day mark, as Jews congregated to pray for Israel's survival.

The funds poured in, surpassing all previous campaigns. Organizations called a moratorium on their usual money-raising drives, and all concentrated on the Israel Emergency Fund run by the United Jewish Appeal. Many communities launched their own campaigns even before they were approached. Illustrations abound on the magnitude and even sacrificial elements of the campaign: a United Jewish Appeal luncheon which netted $15,000,000 in fifteen minutes, individuals who took bank loans or cashed in life insurance policies in order to make their contributions, young children who rang doorbells and donated their savings, contributions from Jewish soldiers in Vietnam. Many were first-time donors, some were non-Jews, and some were from the American Council for Judaism. The International Ladies Garment Workers Union purchased $1,000,000 in Israeli bonds; Mount Sinai Hospital in New York offered to pay the salary of doctors who went to serve in Israel. The results amazed the professional fundraisers and caused a log-jam in tabulating the receipts. By the end of the war (i.e., less than a month's time) over $100,000,000 was raised, and the figure climbed to $180,000,000 before the campaign was closed.

The reaction of American Jews in 1967 has not been analyzed in detail, but observers tend to agree that the Holocaust was the major stimulus. According to one analyst, American Jewry was responding more to the history of the Jews from 1930 on than to Israel alone. Their guilt in the wake of the Holocaust—guilt for not having rescued European Jews, guilt over their own fortuitous survival—led them to interpret Arab designs as a threat to the survival of all Jews, another potential Holocaust. No doubt troubled by accounts of Jewish passivity in Nazi hands, they determined that this time there would at least be resistance. Perhaps too, as one sociologist suggests, in a world gone sour and irrational Israel had emerged as something new and good—something that had to be preserved in order to sustain elementary faith in human endeavor.

Another factor which should not be overlooked is the security of American Jews within the United States. Just because they were more at home in the 1960s than ever before, they could assert their Jewishness more boldly. The generation that came to maturity after World War II was thoroughly acculturated, the product of a pluralistic society that had little experience with anti-Semitism. (The awareness of anti-Semitic expressions by black militants became widespread only after those groups vehemently denounced Israel in 1967. Even then Jewish reaction was more of resentment than fear.) As such it was not beset by the immigrant fear of *mah yomru ha-goyyim?*—What will the gentiles say? The fact that no attempt was made to conceal the tremendous sums raised for Israel, which in prior years would have generated concern as a possible basis for charges of Jewish power, was a case in point. Without any hesitation American Jews also displayed a personal pride in two Israeli leaders, Foreign Minister Abba Eban for his statements before the United Nations and General Moshe Dayan for his direction of the military campaign.

Particularly surprising to the Jewish organizations and to observers of the community was the response of Jewish youth. For years analysts had reported a slackening of Jewish identification and a weakening in commitments to Jewish causes on the part of students and other young people. Developments during the war seriously undermined those findings. Upon the outbreak of hostilities the offices of the Jewish Agency were jammed with young people offering to go to Israel. Military service was not permitted, but they volunteered to fill jobs on the homefront. About eight thousand volunteered, but, since the American government imposed a ban on travel to the area, only five hundred were actually sent. On campuses the academic year was virtually over, but students rallied, wrote petitions and letters, and collected money. Many were jolted by the war into rethinking their previously held positions on pacifism and the Jewish establishment. Somehow they could not fit the Israeli war into their generalized categories or stereotypes. Perhaps others were seeking new causes, since the black nationalist movement was openly inhospitable to Jewish support. Individual statements culled from volunteers also indicated that the war evoked an almost visceral response from those who had affiliations with organized Jewish life—suggesting that feelings of Jewishness were there even if dormant. One letter to the *Village Voice* expressed it as follows:

> I think it must have been this way for many of my generation, that the Israeli-Arab collision was a moment of truth. . . . Two weeks ago, Israel was they; now Israel is we. . . . I will not say that it is only because Israel was in the right during this brief war as I never felt my own country to be in the wars of my own life-time. I will not intellectualize it; I am Jewish; . . . it is a Jewish we. Something happened. I will never again be able to talk about how Judaism is only a religion, and isn't it too bad that there has to be such a thing as a Jewish state. . . . Roots count.[12]

David Ben-Gurion, now Israel's elder statesman, spoke in glowing terms about the idealism shown by American youth. "When they are called upon to help in the creative work in Israel," he added confidently, "they will respond." [13]

The overall Jewish reaction was an ethnic rather than religious display. Jews as a *people* sided with Israel; religious identification made little difference.[14] When the fighting stopped, the secularist and the religious Jew rejoiced together over the reunification of Jerusalem and the repossession of the Wailing Wall.

How permanent the upsurge in Jewish identity will be within the American Jewish community is open to conjecture. Given the intense identification with the Israelis, the latter's victory was a personal triumph for American Jews as well. The effect of the war in enhancing the image of the Jew—the tough fighter, or, as it is said, "the Jew as *goy*," [15] may also have increased group pride within the community. Some reactions evoked by the war have lasted. For example, the aroused Jewish faculty at the country's major universities organized a new pro-Israel group, American Professors for Peace in the Middle East. On the other hand, sociologist Marshall Sklare, who revisited a midwestern Jewish community to compare postwar attitudes with his original findings a decade earlier, concluded that in that city at least, the war had left no major permanent impact.

Zionist leaders found the greatest encouragement for their continued activity in the student response. Increased emphasis was put on youth work and on aliyah. At the seventieth convention of the Zionist Organization of America, held in Jerusalem immediately after the war, Emanuel Neumann stated that every American Jewish family should be represented by at least one member in Israel. When Prime Minister Eshkol told the American delegates that "Zionism and *aliyah* are one and the same thing," his remarks were warmly received—a far cry from the reactions to Ben-Gurion's similar statements fifteen years before. Zionists also believed that their new commitment to an educational program within the community was amply vindicated by surveys which revealed that most of the young volunteers in 1967 had previously received some form of Jewish training. The twin pillars of aliyah and diaspora education underlay the ZOA pledge in 1967:

We, as Zionists, will continue to strive for a meaningful and creative Jewish survival in the Diaspora and to give to Israel our understanding, our cooperation, our untiring devotion. Together with our brethren in Israel we shall move forward to ensure the survival of the Jewish people and the fulfillment of its destiny.[16]

10

In Retrospect

Seventy-five years after the First Zionist Congress it has become commonplace in the United States to assume that as a group American Jews are Zionists. Friend and critic alike use the word *Zionist* today to mean some degree of concern, interest, or identification with the State of Israel. American Zionism connotes, and rightly so, something more than affiliation with a Zionist organization. It is the end product of stimuli from three sources which have influenced the American Jewish community during the twentieth century: the needs of that community itself, the needs of world Jewry, the demands and opinions of American society.

The East European Jews brought with them into the United States a deeply rooted Jewish heritage. If asked to explain what their Jewishness meant, they would have defined it in religious and nationalist terms. It denoted a ritualized faith, a peoplehood or nationality which in the course of history gave rise to a distinctive culture, and a destiny which linked them to Jews all over the world. Most of them could not, and would not, consciously give up their heritage; to stop being Jewish would mean to stop being. But they needed to adapt that heritage to their new surroundings, to reconcile old loyalties with a new faith. For Jews embraced their Americanism with a passion; America was their *goldene medinah* ("golden land"). Furthermore, they sought to fit their heritage to the secularist currents of thought which they had begun to imbibe in Eastern Europe. Most could not exchange their Jewish identity for universalist causes. Classical Reform, which set Jews apart as a religion until their message of the fatherhood of God and the brotherhood of man would be accepted by the nations, was meaningless to them. Even those who tried socialism could not submerge their Jewish interests in the struggle of the proletariat. When

142

socialist parties paid no attention to specifically Jewish issues, like pogroms or immigration, Jews often broke away.

The Zionist idea, in varying degrees of intensity, was a natural alternative. It fused religious tradition with secularism, as, in fact, most immigrants were doing in their daily life-styles. In spirit it was traditionalist enough to engage the sympathy of most religious Jews, yet it was sufficiently secularist for the totally nonreligious who still wanted a place within the community. The first-and second-generation immigrants also found emotional release in Zionism. It eased the trauma of being thrown into an alien society and being buffeted about and frequently rejected by that society.

But Zionism was more than a temporary phenomenon or service station on the road to assimilation. Indeed, Zionist sentiment became stronger with the third and fourth generations even though they no longer had the close familial ties of their ancestors with the Yishuv. Today its pervasiveness can be measured in numerous ways. Israel is the favorite philanthropic cause—and its problems the ongoing preoccupation—of Jewish organizations, synagogues and schools, sermons and books. Israel continues to attract waves of tourists, and its artifacts and souvenirs are conspicuous in American homes. Jewish organizations maintain offices in Israel, and American Zionist groups build housing projects there. Rabbinical seminaries, dedicated to the preservation of Judaism in the diaspora, maintain centers in Israel and encourage students to spend a year of their course of study in Jerusalem. On another level, a growing number of Jews, and not necessarily those tied to Zionist organizations, now invoke Israel as a personal option. If living in the United States—with crime in the streets or occupational quotas for minorities (which can be anti-Jewish quotas)—becomes unbearable, Israel might serve as an asylum. They do not really plan aliyah, but they are groping for a way out of their disillusionment. They turn to Israel, just as some of their uprooted immigrant forefathers turned to Zionism, to ease the shocks of American living.

Support for Israel has become the lowest common denominator of American Jewish group identity. One sociologist suggests that the community judges nonsupport of the Jewish state to be a more significant deviation than intermarriage. He adds that Jews denounce the New Left primarily because of its anti-Israel posture, more than for its revolt against Jewish moral precepts or its readiness to use violence. To many, Jews who belong to the New Left are outright traitors to their people. Pockets of ultra-Orthodox Hasidim in the United States who still oppose a secular Jewish state evoke contempt rather than condemnation. Unlike the Jews of the New Left the Hasidim are quiescent, totally divorced from the American mainstream, and curiosities rather than rebels.

The major force responsible for the growth of Jewish nationalist sentiment was the Holocaust. Never in their gloomiest moments had Zionist thinkers forecast such destruction, but for the postwar generation it served to vindicate the Zionist interpretation of history. Anti-Semitism was endemic to Christian society; individuals could find acceptance but never the group. Whether in fact, or by divine arrangement, or merely in the minds of the gentiles, Jews were part of a group whose destiny *as a group* could not be escaped. Youth couples its wariness of the outside world with a determination to fight back. Jewish college students discussing the Holocaust are puzzled more by the relative absence of resistance on the part of Hitler's victims than by the apathy of civilized society. The same students (not necessarily members of the Jewish Defense League) sneer at Jewish organizations that advise Jews to lend their help to affirmative-action quotas. Their intense reaction to the Six-Day War reflected the determination to avoid another betrayal at the hands of the non-Jews or at least to go down fighting.

Underlying this post-Holocaust climate of opinion is the consciousness, perhaps visceral more than rational, that in a non-Jewish society Jews are always Jews among gentiles. Only in a Jewish society are they men among men. It made no difference whether they willingly discarded their particularist habits and repudiated their particularist aims. To society they were still Jews. Even in the United States there was not a completely open society where Jews could be of that society and yet retain their differences. Many did gain full acceptance, but that usually went along with submerging their Jewish identity. Neither Jews nor their fellow Americans had learned to accept Jewish differences comfortably. Universalism also stopped short with Jews. The Jew who throws himself into humanistic causes—civil rights, social action, New Left—is still pushing to obliterate the differences that set him apart from other human beings. To free himself from the condition of Jewishness, which is the prime divider, he is ready to serve suffering humanity and, if necessary, fight against Jewish interests. But the fact that an Abbie Hoffman can still be called a Zionist may prove that no matter to what lengths the humanists go, they cannot escape their Jewishness.

The American Jewish response to the Zionist idea always took its cue from the American scene. When Wilson talked of national self-determination, when Truman took up the cause of the displaced persons, when non-

Jews expounded the theme of cultural pluralism, and when the American public grew accustomed to minority demands, overt Jewish support for Zionism rose. Conversely, when the country recoiled into a narrow nationalist posture during the twenties, or when anti-Semites in the thirties attacked Jews for their separatism, organized Zionist strength declined. It never evaporated entirely, for if confined to philanthropy or refugeeism it was unobjectionable. Zionists employed a vocabulary and imagery aimed at making the movement more palatable to Americans and, in turn, to Jews: Zionism stood for democracy and social reform; the early Zionists were like the Pilgrim Fathers; Zionism was progressivism; like America's humanitarian diplomacy, Zionism worked for the persecuted in Europe; a Jewish state served the purposes of Cold War containment.

Organized Zionists operated like other pressure groups in American politics. From the thirties, when England considered partition and then promulgated the White Paper, Zionists worked in sustained fashion to swing official opinion to their side. They concentrated on men of influence and on nerve-centers of public opinion—politicians, lawmakers, the press, labor leaders, Christian clergy. In the main, the Zionists succeeded in winning congressional support. Their cause crossed party lines and was supported by both conservatives and liberals. But since control of foreign policy, from Franklin Roosevelt's time on, passed more and more into the hands of the executive, congressional sympathy was never decisive in itself. The executive was less malleable. Presidents and presidential hopefuls mouthed solicitous phrases, but even if the president personally favored Zionism, as Truman and Johnson did, his choices were qualified by multiple diplomatic and political considerations. Within the State Department, particularly in the faceless lower echelons which made day-to-day policy and continued in office irrespective of election results, anti-Zionism, reinforced by the traditional anti-Semitic bent of career diplomacy, was a fact of life since pre–World War I days.

Official United States policy toward Zionism and Israel did not follow the guidelines set by the benevolent Wilson. But American Jews found it easier to go along with indifference and hostility than to risk an open confrontation with the government. In the twenties, their insecurity as a new immigrant group faced by eruptions of anti-Semitism kept them quiet. During the Roosevelt era they were lulled by their loyalty to the New Deal. They were also sidetracked by the problems foisted upon them by the depression and by the rapidly multiplying anti-Semitic organizations. Even during the Sinai War of 1956 the Jews did not contradict the government's denunciation of Israeli aggression. Put on the defensive, they tried to explain why Israel had resorted to force, and they worked to prevent the imposition of sanctions on the Jewish state. Zionists and their allies challenged the government in a sustained campaign only during the years 1943–48, when they were goaded into action by the knowledge of the death camps.

Since the United States in the post-1948 era always affirmed a commitment to Israel's survival, American Jews have been uninhibited about showing their ties with the Jewish state. But equally important is the fact that the more Americanized the Jews have become, the more assertive they are in expressing themselves as Jews. The children of the immigrants would not have dreamed of wearing skullcaps, even at the College of the City of New York, but the grandchildren do, and on the most prestigious campuses of the country. (Skullcaps, some wearers explain, are now symbols of belonging to a group and not merely signs of Orthodox ritual.) In response to student demand, Jewish studies programs have sprung up at numerous colleges and universities. Princeton, once the symbol of establishment exclusiveness, informs prospective Jewish applicants where they can obtain kosher food.

As Americanization proceeded, the Jews were influenced in two ways. They became more sensitive to the ultimate dividing line between them and general society, and they became sufficiently rooted in that society to make their feelings known. If there was something inherent in being Jewish which kept them apart from non-Jews, it made more sense to develop their Jewishness unashamedly and for their own comfort.

Since the creation of the Jewish state even more than before 1948, the synagogues have constituted the bedrock of Zionist support. In that respect, too, the form of Jewish nationalist expression was shaped by American influences. Since America tolerated deviations in religion but would not countenance separatist subcultures, the synagogues grew in importance. Increasingly Americanized, from language to architecture, they took on ethnic as well as religious functions. With their schools, lecture series, cub scout groups, and basketball teams, synagogues have become much more than houses of worship. Today they are cultural centers whose major thrust is the survival of the Jewish group. In their extrareligious activities, Israel and peoplehood command a central position. Even within the religious service itself, the weekly sermons and periodic fund-raising appeals sharpen the nationalist focus.

Synagogal sponsorship has imbued nationalist activities with religious meaning. If a synagogue's school teaches Zionism, or imparts a Zionist flavor to lessons in history and ritual, a nexus between nationalism and religion is established. For the membership at large that is perfectly acceptable. About sixty percent of American Jews are affiliated with synagogues. Most are probably no more ritualistically inclined than the unaffiliated, but they join in order to express an ethnic as well as religious identity. Since their objectives are serviced in so many ways by the synagogue, they come to assume that identification with the Jewish people and the Jewish state is as much a part of Jewish ritual as a seder on Passover. As "church-goers" modern Jews are solidly American, and as "church-goers" they preserve their ethnicity. American Judiasm has fused the religious and nationalist elements of the tradition under a religious rubric and Americanized format.

An ambivalence characterized American Jews. On the one hand they knew that the destiny which linked them to Jews all over the world could not be escaped in the United States. At the same time they believed, and worked to make that belief come true, that with the arrival of Jews in the United States Jewish history in the diaspora had turned a corner.

From its very beginnings American Zionism absolved its corner of the diaspora from the Herzlian interpretation of history and its followers from the commitment of aliyah. American Zionism has meant the creation and maintenance of a state peopled by others, largely those who could not find acceptance elsewhere. True, American society had its own dividing line between Jew and gentile, but the obstacles to be overcome were far less formidable than what Jews had experienced in two millennia. There was no established church shaping government policy, no entrenched aristocracy or military caste (a Jew had been in the first class to graduate West Point), no official quota on how many Jews could work at certain trades or professions, no federal restrictions on voting or office-holding, no major political parties propagating anti-Semitism. In the years following World War II significant strides were made in tearing down the last bastions of WASP exclusiveness: the executive suite in industry, fraternities and clubs, university teaching and administrative posts. The promise of America had been largely fulfilled for the vast majority of American Jews. They too affirmed the idea imbedded in American tradition since the eighteenth century that the New World, by living example, would contradict the decadence and impurities of the Old.

Since America was different, American Zionism was too. In large measure it was a philanthropic movement on behalf of unfortunate Jews. It also offered American Jews a way of expressing their ties, past and present, with Jewry wherever it existed. As a sociological force within the American Jewish community it contributed to the maturation of the East European immigrants and propelled them to positions of communal leadership. Simultaneously it helped to weld the various strands of the community into a cohesive whole.

Analysts have stressed the psychological impact of the Zionist idea on American Jews. Even if they never planned to settle in Palestine or Israel, Zionism gave them a positive cause to fight for. It was daring and creative, different from the typical welfare or defense activities which were ad hoc responses to the needs of everyday diaspora living. As such, Zionism imbued its followers with feelings of self-confidence, and it sparked new interest in Jewish culture. The Zionist idea helped to modify the image of the Jew in his own eyes and those of the world. No longer was he the eternal wanderer, the easy target for humiliation and persecution, but he was the fighter seeking to repossess his homeland. When the state was finally established, Jews became a "normal" people. They were no longer the survivors of an archaic civilization. They had paratroopers, plastics factories, and atomic generators as well as rabbis and scholars. Respect for the Jew increased, and to that extent anti-Semitism was undermined. For the Jew the change was more dramatic. Having reached the level of "all the nations," he was prouder and more comfortable with his Jewishness. Self-hatred, a common affliction among Jews ever since the Enlightenment, receded. Jewish dependence on Israel for emotional well-being was reflected in the intensity of the reaction to the Six-Day War. A Jewish defeat would hardly have spelled the extermination of world Jewry or the immediate end to diaspora Judaism. But it would have left a deep psychological void underscoring the futility of the Jewish struggle to survive.

Despite their secularist life-styles, many American Jews view Israel from a religious perspective. They do not wrestle with theology or purport to articulate their sentiments in religious terms, but Israel to them is still the Holy Land. They see the state as the fulfillment of the divine commitment to the Jews or as the vindication of Jewish suffering, which culminated in the deaths of six million. Jews who do not observe the dietary laws expect the food supplied by Israeli institutions to be kosher. American Jews are bitter about crime in New York but stunned by news of thefts and rapes in Tel Aviv. Like their ancestors who supported Jewish schools and scholars in Palestine long before Zionism, modern Jews retain the belief that the Holy Land is an essential part of salvation. Accordingly, Jewish life there, which stores up grace for the entire people, needs to be purer and more Jewish.

The religious and psychological importance of the Zionist idea for American Jews could, however, lead to a progressive weakening of American Judaism. Professor Jacob Neusner succinctly analyzes the question that troubles American Jewish religious leaders: How long can American Judaism live off the cultural and military bounty of Israel? If American Judaism continues to draw its spiritual sustenance from a distant land rather than from native sources, and if it persists in substituting ethnicity for religion, its own health is jeopardized. Neusner and others say that American Jews must be awakened to the legitimacy and needs of diaspora Judaism. They must recognize that the Zionist idea is only one part of Judaism and Israel only one segment of the Jewish people.

As long as the Zionist idea continues to service the culture and psyche of American Jews, the latter will be bound up with Israel and Israelis. But the two centers of Jewry are different communities with separate sets of needs. Aside from the demands of security, which overshadow its economy and politics, Israel faces major social problems. The tension between the Western Jews and the newer Levantine and North African immigrants is one; the rapid and unplanned burgeoning of cities, with their attendant social ills and their threat to the socialist dream, is another. The idyllic conditions projected by Theodor Herzl in *Altneuland,* his utopian tract, which followed *The Jewish State,* are far from actuality.

Equally serious to Israeli officials and intellectual leaders is the "dejudaization" of the native Israelis. Not only are most nonreligious or antireligious, but consciously or unconsciously many draw a line between Israeli and Jew. They reject diaspora Judaism and feel contempt for the self-consciousness and wariness of the diaspora mentality. Extremists who call themselves Canaanites divorce themselves totally from all aspects of Jewish history that took place outside Palestine. Israeli youth is poorly educated in modern Jewish history. They understand little of the significance of nineteenth-and twentieth-century developments, even with respect to the Holocaust or to Zionist history up to their state. The more pervasive that ignorance, the weaker their sense of kinship with other Jews.

Israel appreciates the economic help it gets from the United States and from American Jews, but like most recipients it is resentful too. The number of Israelis who have settled in affluent America since the creation of the state surpasses that of American Jews whom Israel has been able to attract. It is easy for Israelis to attribute their failure to win and keep American *olim* to the dependence of Americans on material comforts. They shut their eyes to the psychological difficulties of uprooting and to the numerous petty obstacles posed by Israeli conditions. Nor does the stereotyped American Jewish contributor, who jaunts around the country from his base at the Hilton Hotels, behaving as if his dollars have bought him a share of the country, evoke Israeli respect.

When Israelis consider American Jews, they are struck by what seem to be gross inconsistencies. The Americans define themselves as a religion but are in fact nonobservant; they call themselves Zionists but refuse to settle in Israel. Israelis fail to grasp the way in which the American environment has shaped the development of the Jewish community there. Since they themselves have no religious option but the rigorous Orthodoxy imposed by the politically powerful religious parties, they are unfamiliar with American Reform and Conservatism. When ignorance is coupled with Orthodox intransigence on Conservative and Reform legal ceremonies (e.g., marriages and divorces), the gap between the two communities grows wider. Differences over religion point up a more serious obstacle to a mutually beneficial relationship: Israelis cannot yet see how they can be spiritually enriched by what has been created in the diaspora.

Just because Jews are a religious-national group, neither religion alone nor nationalism alone can perpetuate the Jewish heritage in its totality. That applies to Israel as well as to the American Jewish community. Since Israel and the United States are the major centers of contemporary Jewish life, the survival of Jews and Judaism for the foreseeable future depends upon both. The kind of survival will be determined by how well the two can develop their Jewish resources independently and how they can enrich each other at the same time. Perhaps in time the Zionist idea will develop a new dynamic that will enable it to continue as a productive and unifying force for both communities.

NOTES TO PROLOGUE

1. Arthur Hertzberg, ed., *The Zionist Idea* (New York, 1960), p. 15.
2. Alex Bein, *Theodore Herzl* (New York, 1970), pp. 115–16.
3. *Universal Jewish Encyclopedia*, s. v. "Basel Program."
4. Walter Laqueur, *A History of Zionism* (New York, 1972), p. 89.

NOTES TO CHAPTER 1—A PATTERN IS SET

1. Bernard G. Richards, "Zionism in the United States," in Israel Cohen, *The Zionist Movement*, rev. ed. (New York, 1946), p. 326.
2. Frank E. Manuel, *The Realities of American-Palestine Relations* (Washington, 1949), p. 2.
3. Union of American Hebrew Congregations, *Proceedings* 5:4002.
4. Joseph Tabachnick, "American Jewish Reaction to the First Zionist Congress," *Herzl Year Book* 5 (1963): 61.
5. C. Bezalel Sherman, *Labor Zionism in America* (New York, 1957), p. 7.
6. The labor group was the first to involve Zionists in American Jewish education when they introduced the Jewish *Folkshulen* in 1910. Mirroring the nationalist and socialist outlook of their founders, the schools encouraged greater interest in Jewish cultural and literary endeavors.
7. Stephen S. Wise, "The Beginnings of American Zionism," *Jewish Frontier* 14 (August 1947): 7.
8. The Kehillah united a wide range of Jewish organizations in New York for the purpose of dealing with communal needs of education, philanthropy, labor, and crime-fighting.
9. Hertzberg, *The Zionist Idea*, p. 507.
10. Emma Lazarus, *An Epistle to the Hebrews* (New York, 1900), p. 41.
11. Gottheil Papers (Zionist Archives): Herzl to Gottheil, December 19, 1899; Gottheil to Actions Committee, January 12, 1900.

NOTES TO CHAPTER 2—ZIONISM AS PROGRESSIVISM

1. Louis Lipsky, *A Gallery of Zionist Profiles* (New York, 1956), p. 155.
2. Jacob De Haas, *Louis D. Brandeis* (New York, 1929), pp. 161–62. See also Melvin I. Urofsky. *A Mind of One Piece* (New York, 1971), ch. 5.
3. *Maccabaean*, March, September 1917.
4. Facsimile reproduced in *Universal Jewish Encyclopedia*, 2:47.
5. Selig Adler, "Backgrounds of American Policy toward Zion," in *Israel: Its Role in Civilization*, ed. Moshe Davis (New York, 1956), p. 275.
6. *American Hebrew*, February 1, 1918.
7. *Maccabaean*, August, September, 1918.

NOTES TO CHAPTER 3—POSTWAR DECLINE

1. De Haas, *Louis D. Brandeis*, p. 233
2. George Berlin, "The Brandeis-Weizmann Dispute," *American Jewish Historical Quarterly* 60 (September 1970): 40.
3. Stephen S. Wise, *Challenging Years* (New York, 1949), p. 208.
4. Adler, "American Policy toward Zion," p. 276.
5. *New Palestine*, April 15, 1921.
6. Lewisohn, esp. *The Island Within* (1928) and his autobiography, *Upstream* (1922); Samuel, *You Gentiles* (1924) and *I, the Jew* (1927).
7. One source, *A Century of U. S. Aliya*, points out the difficulties in determin-

ing how many Americans settled in Palestine. Its estimate for the period 1918–31 is over four thousand. That includes city-dwellers as well as agricultural pioneers. It does not take account of those who returned to the United States (possibly as many as thirty percent).

8. Samuel Halperin, *The Political World of American Zionism* (Detroit, 1961), p. 13.

9. Carl H. Voss, ed., *Stephen S. Wise: Servant of the People* (Philadelphia, 1969), pp. 167–68.

10. Ibid.

NOTES TO CHAPTER 4—YEARS OF CRISIS

1. *Strangers and Natives* (New York, 1968), pp. 170–71.

2. *Proceedings of the National Conference for Palestine,* January 20 and 21, 1935, pp. 22–27.

3. Samuel Grand, "A History of Zionist Youth Organizations in the United States from Their Inception to 1940" (dissertation, Columbia University, 1958), pp. 192–93.

4. For the same reason B'nai B'rith became increasingly more sympathetic to Zionism.

5. *American Jewish Year Book,* 38 (1936–37): 619.

6. Literally, the "night of broken glass," when hundreds of synagogues and Jewish shops were burned and thousands of Jews placed in concentration camps.

7. Naomi W. Cohen, *Not Free to Desist* (Philadelphia, 1972), p. 175.

8. *New Palestine,* July 12, 1937.

9. "The Voice of Christian America," *Proceedings of the National Conference on Palestine,* March 9, 1944, p. 29.

NOTES TO CHAPTER 5—HERZL REAFFIRMED

1. *Contemporary Jewish Record* 2 (May–June 1939): 63.

2. Selig Adler, *The Isolationist Impulse* (New York, 1961), p. 252.

3. The Revisionist party was formed in 1923 in protest against Weizmann's moderate policies. It represented a more aggressive nationalism and emphasized political agitation over practical Zionism. Its leader, the colorful Vladimir Jabotinsky, had long been the protagonist of a Jewish army, and he was responsible for the Jewish Legion of World War I. In the thirties the Revisionists broke away from the Yishuv's defense force, Haganah, and with other right-wing and militant groups set up their own force, Irgun. Unlike the Haganah, the Irgun resorted to terrorism in campaigns against the Arabs and the British.

4. Yehuda Bauer, *From Diplomacy to Resistance* (Philadelphia, 1970), p. 72.

5. May 1940, p. 5.

6. Arthur D. Morse, *While Six Million Died* (New York, 1967), p. 89.

7. Henry L. Feingold, *The Politics of Rescue* (New Brunswick, N. J., 1970), p. 244.

8. *The Memoirs of Cordell Hull, 2 vols.* (New York, 1948), 2: 1536.

9. Cohen, *Not Free to Desist,* p. 231.

10. *New Palestine,* January 31, 1941.

11. Ibid., September 19, 1941.

12. ESCO Foundation, *Palestine: A Study of Jewish, Arab, and British Policies,* 2 vols. (New Haven, 1947), 2: 1084–85.

13. May 15, 1942.

14. "Zionist Policy in the Post-War Period," *Palestine Year Book* 3 (1947–48): 33–34.

15. Joseph B. Schechtman, *The United States and the Jewish State Movement* (New York, 1966), p. 70.
16. Ibid., p. 74.
17. Ibid., p. 26.
18. Ibid., p. 43.
19. Abba Hillel Silver, *Vision and Victory* (New York, 1949), p. 71.

NOTES TO CHAPTER 6—THE REBIRTH OF ISRAEL

1. Halperin, *Political World of American Zionism*, p. 40.
2. American Jewish Conference, *The Jewish Position at the United Nations Conference on International Organization* (New York, 1945), p. 12.
3. Harry S. Truman, *Memoirs: Years of Trial and Hope* (New York, 1965), p. 159.
4. Richard Crossman, *Palestine Mission* (New York, 1947), pp. 31, 38.
5. Irwin Oder, "The United States and the Palestine Mandate, 1920–48" (dissertation, Columbia University, 1956), p. 420.
6. Stephen S. Wise, *Personal Letters*, ed. J. W. Polier and J. W. Wise (New York, 1956), p. 271.
7. Schechtman, *U. S. and the Jewish State Movement*, pp. 182, 184.
8. Silver, *Vision and Victory*, p. 119.
9. Schechtman, *U. S. and the Jewish State Movement*, p. 180.
10. Ian J. Bickerton, "President Truman's Recognition of Israel," *American Jewish Historical Quarterly* 58 (December 1968): 201.
11. Silver, *Vision and Victory*, pp. 146–47.
12. David Horowitz, *State in the Making* (New York, 1953), p. 263.
13. J. C. Hurewitz, *The Struggle for Palestine* (New York, 1950), p. 305.
14. Bickerton, "President Truman's Recognition of Israel," p. 215.
15. Ibid., p. 220.
16. Chaim Weizmann, *Trial and Error*, 2 vols. (Philadelphia, 1949), 2: 474.
17. Bernard Postal and Henry W. Levy, *And the Hills Shouted for Joy* (Philadelphia, 1973), p. 185.

NOTES TO CHAPTER 7—COLD WAR POLITICS

1. Kirk H. Porter and Donald B. Johnson, comps., *National Party Platforms* (Urbana, Ill., 1961), p. 440.
2. *New Palestine*, July 23, 1948.
3. Only the American Council for Judaism remained outspokenly anti-Zionist. Upon the creation of the state, a faction in the council saw no reason to continue the organization and resigned. Those who stayed were the more extreme anti-Zionists, and consequently the council's attacks became increasingly more vitriolic.
4. Henry S. Commager, ed., *Documents of American History*, 7th ed. (New York, 1963), 2: 526.
5. AJC Vertical Files, Israel and the U.S.: American Zionist Council memo, June 1, 1951.
6. AJC Vertical Files, Middle East and the U.S./Zionist Organizations: American Zionist Council, Memorandum on Aid to the Near East, April 7, 1952.
7. Harry N. Howard, *U. S. Policy in the Near East, South Asia, and Africa, 1954*, Dept. of State Publ. 5801, pp. 22–23.
8. November 15, 1955.
9. AJC Vertical Files, Middle East (Egypt and Israel): resolution of presidents of organizations, November 27, 1956.

10. Herman Finer, *Dulles over Suez* (Chicago, 1964), pp. 482–83.

11. *American Zionist,* March 1957.

12. John C. Campbell, *Defense of the Middle East,* 2d ed. (New York, 1960), p. 202.

13. AJC Vertical Files, Middle East/Boycott, Arab/A. J. Cong.: I. Goldstein to J. F. Dulles, July 10, 1956.

14. *American Jewish Year Book* 66 (1965): 306.

15. Ibid., 67 (1966): 273–74.

16. One example was the sale and distribution of Arab propaganda by the National Renaissance party, a New York-based Nazi group.

17. *Near East Report,* August 25, 1964.

18. *Congressional Record,* 86th Cong., 2d sess., 1960, p. 8976.

NOTES TO CHAPTER 8—REDEFINING THE TIES

1. *The Jew in American Literature* (New York, 1966), p. 216.

2. The divisions within the Zionist movement—religious, labor, revisionist— were the bases for the creation of political parties in the Yishuv. Their political programs, in turn, shaped the various Zionist groups outside Palestine.

3. The congress, the first to be held after the establishment of the state, resolved: "The task of Zionism is to strengthen the State of Israel, to gather the exiles in the Land of Israel, and to guarantee the unity of the Jewish people." *Encyclopedia of Zionism and Israel,* s. v. "Congress, Zionist."

4. *Session of the Zionist General Council,* Jerusalem, December 24–31, 1953, p. 116.

5. *American Jewish Year Book* 52 (1951): 115.

6. Ibid. 62 (1961): 195.

7. *New Palestine,* May 18, 1948.

8. Judd L. Teller, "American Zionists Move toward Clarity," *Commentary* 12 (November 1951): 445.

9. The text of the Ben-Gurion–Blaustein statement appears in American Jewish Committee, *In Vigilant Brotherhood* (New York, 1964), pp. 64–69.

10. UJA collections amounted to $150,000,000 in 1948 but then began to fall, and for most years thereafter (except for the Suez crisis) they reached only forty to fifty percent of that amount. With the Six-Day War the trend was reversed, and annual contributions climbed to new heights. Charles S. Liebman, *The Ambivalent American Jew* (Philadelphia, 1973), p. 91.

11. Accounts differ on numbers. There is reason to question the accuracy of the official rolls, which listed only three hundred volunteers from the United States.

12. David Breslau, ed., *Arise and Build* (New York, 1961), p. 84.

13. Mendel Kohansky, "A Report from the Zionist Congress," *Jewish Frontier* 23 (June 1956): 14.

14. "Two Worlds—Two Responses," *Congress Weekly,* May 24, 1954.

15. Benno Weiser, "Ben-Gurion's Dispute with American Zionists," *Commentary* 18 (August 1954): 99–100.

16. David Ben-Gurion, *Rebirth and Destiny of Israel* (New York, 1954), p. 539.

17. Teller, "American Zionists Move toward Clarity," p. 446.

18. Both sides overstepped the dividing lines on occasion, and interest became interference. In the winter of 1959–60, in the wake of anti-Semitic incidents in the United States and other countries, Israel took the position of spokesman for world Jewry. On the other side, seven American Jewish organizations appealed to the

Israeli government in 1964 to resist demands by the Orthodox for policies that would restrict religious freedom in that country.

19. Mordecai M. Kaplan, *A New Zionism,* 2d ed. (New York, 1959), p. 99.

20. Ibid., pp. 12, 42.

21. *American Zionist* 51 (September 1960): 12.

NOTES TO CHAPTER 9—THE SIX-DAY WAR

1. Theodore H. White, *The Making of the President 1968* (New York, 1969), p. 12.

2. *American Jewish Year Book* 69 (1968): 165, 169.

3. Ibid., p. 170.

4. Ibid., pp. 155, 172.

5. Ibid., p. 174.

6. *Congressional Record,* 90th Cong., 1st sess., 1967, p. 14851.

7. *New York Post,* June 10, 1967.

8. Richard L. Rubenstein, *Israel, Zionism and the New Left* (New York, 1969), pp. 7, 29.

9. Theodore Draper, *Israel and World Politics* (New York, 1968), p. 117.

10. Judith H. Banki, *Christian Reactions to the Middle East Crisis* (New York, 1968), p. 6.

11. *Report on Activities in North America, April 1, 1964–December 31, 1967* (Submitted to 27th Zionist Congress), p. 7.

12. *American Jewish Year Book* 69 (1968): 211.

13. ZOA, *The 70th Jubilee Convention, July 19–26, 1967,* p. 48.

14. A Unitarian church in a midwestern suburb was the only church of that community to raise funds for Israel, for a good number of its members were of Jewish origin.

15. Robert Alter, "Israel and the Intellectuals," *A Commentary Report: American Reactions to the Six Day War* (New York, 1967), p. 7.

16. ZOA, *70th Jubilee Convention,* pp. 17, 63.

Notes on Sources

Only direct quotations and some abstruse points have been documented in the text. The following titles indicate the materials that were of greatest value in preparing this book. They also serve as suggestions for further reading and research.*

General Accounts

On Zionist thought, see especially Ben Halpern, *The Idea of the Jewish State* (1969), and Arthur Hertzberg, ed., *The Zionist Idea* (1959). For the outstanding events and personalities of the Zionist movement, see Walter Laqueur, *A History of Zionism* (1972); ESCO Foundation, *Palestine: A Study of Jewish, Arab and British Policies* (1947); J. C. Hurewitz, *The Struggle for Palestine* (1950). Palestine and Israel are set on the broader canvas of international diplomacy in the accounts by Howard Sachar: *The Emergence of the Middle East, 1914–1924* (1969) and *Europe Leaves the Middle East, 1936–1954* (1972).

Major trends in the evolution of the American Jewish community are interpreted by Nathan Glazer in *American Judaism* (1972) and "Social Characteristics of American Jews" (in *The Jews: Their History, Culture and Religion,* ed. Louis Finkelstein, 1960); Rufus Learsi, *The Jews in America* (1972); Oscar Handlin, *Adventure in Freedom* (1954); Judd L. Teller, *Strangers and Natives* (1968); and Naomi W. Cohen, *Not Free to Desist* (1972).

Extremely useful studies on the nature of American Zionism are Samuel Halperin, *The Political World of American Zionism* (1961); Yonathan Shapiro, *Leadership of the American Zionist Organization, 1897–1930* (1971); and Judd L. Teller, "Zionism, Israel and American

---

* The following abbreviations have been used in this section:
  AJA—American Jewish Archives
  AJHQ—American Jewish Historical Quarterly
  AJYB—American Jewish Year Book
  JSS—Jewish Social Studies
  PYB—Palestine Year Book
  PAJHS—Publication(s) of the American Jewish Historical Society

Jewry" (in *The American Jew: A Reappraisal*, ed. Oscar Janowsky, 1964). American diplomatic policies affecting Zionism are ably discussed by Frank Manuel, *Realities of American-Palestine Relations* (1949); Selig Adler, "Backgrounds of American Policy toward Zion" (in *Israel: Its Role in Civilization*, ed. Moshe Davis, 1956); Carl J. Friedrich, *American Policy toward Palestine* (1944); and Irwin Oder, "The United States and the Palestine Mandate, 1920–48" (Unpublished dissertation, Columbia University, 1956). For the decade preceding statehood, see Joseph B. Schechtman, *The United States and the Jewish State Movement* (1966). Robert Silverberg, *If I Forget Thee, O Jerusalem* (1970), is a spirited popular account of American Jewish interest in Palestine. P. E. Lapide, *A Century of U.S. Aliya* (1961), is sketchy but, as the only such summary of the subject, important. A typescript in the Zionist Archives, "Fifty Years of American Zionism," adds factual details on projects initiated by American Zionists but is disappointing for its lack of interpretation.

Memoirs and biographies enrich the study of the Zionist movement. Of special value are those of Chaim Weizmann, Stephen S. Wise, Louis D. Brandeis, and Judah Magnes. For the interpretations of an active participant, see Louis Lipsky, *A Gallery of Zionist Profiles* (1956) and *Thirty Years of American Zionism* (1927).

Zionist newspapers and other periodicals are of particular value. See especially the *Maccabaean, New Palestine, American Zionist, Jewish Frontier,* and *Congress Weekly.* A useful index to periodical and pamphlet literature, *Palestine and Zionism,* was prepared by the Zionist Archives for the years 1946–55. The annual AJYB remains the most important source for background information.

In addition to the general accounts, newspaper files, and organizational material, the following works pertain to specific chapters.

Chapter 1

The surveys by Israel Cohen, *The Zionist Movement* (1946), and Nahum Sokolow, *History of Zionism, 1600–1918* (1919), include references to American and American Jewish interest in Palestine before Herzl. Other detailed accounts of pre–World War I activitiy are found in Isidore S. Meyer, ed., *Early History of Zionism in America* (1958); Marnin Feinstein, *American Zionism 1884–1904* (1965); David de Sola Pool, "Early Relations between Palestine and American Jewry" (in *Brandeis Avukah Annual of 1932,* ed. Joseph Shubow); Max J. Kohler, "Some Early American Zionist Projects," *PAJHS* 8 (1900); Salo W. Baron and Jeannette M.

Baron, "Palestinian Messengers in America, 1849–79," *JSS* 5 (1943). The *Herzl Year Book,* 5 (1963) and 6 (1965), includes articles on early Zionism in different geographic areas of the United States and on popular reaction to the Zionist movement.

Moses Rischin's *The Promised City* (1962) portrays the background and concerns of the East European immigrants. The views of Jewish labor on Zionism appear in C. Bezalel Sherman's *Labor Zionism in America* (1957, while aspects of religious Zionist thought are treated in P. Churgin and L. Gellman, eds., *Mizrachi, Jubilee Publication of the Mizrachi Organization of America* (1936). Conservative Judaism and Zionism is examined in Moshe Davis, *The Emergence of Conservative Judaism* (1963) and Herbert Parzen, "Conservative Judaism and Zionism, 1896–1922," *JSS* 23 (1961). Reform opposition to Zionism is analyzed in Naomi W. Cohen, "The Reaction of Reform Judaism in America to Political Zionism, 1897–1922," *PAJHS* 40 (1951).

Pertinent memoirs of early Zionist activists include Julius Haber, *The Odyssey of an American Zionist* (1956); Bernard Horwich, *My First Eighty Years* (1939); and Meyer Weisgal, *So Far* (1971). See also the biographies of Gustav Gottheil, Bernhard Felsenthal, Henrietta Szold, and Solomon Schechter.

Aspects of special projects for the development of Palestine are treated in Abraham Goldberg, "Zionism in America" (in *Theodor Herzl, A Memorial,* ed. M. Weisgal, 1929), and Alex Bein, "American Settlement in Israel" (in *Israel: Its Role in Civilization,* ed. Moshe Davis, 1956).

The pamphlets published by the FAZ are very helpful for the ideology of prewar Zionism. Other contemporary sources are Jacob De Haas, *Zionism: Why and Wherefore* (1902); Judah L. Magnes, *Evidences of Jewish Nationality* (1908); and Richard J. H. Gottheil, *Zionism* (1914). See also Naomi W. Cohen, "The ,Maccabaean's Message: A Study in American Zionism Until World War I," *JSS* 18(1956).

Chapter 2

Brandeis's Zionist activities are discussed most recently by Melvin I. Urofsky, *A Mind of One Piece* (1971). See also Leo Shubow, "Jacob De Haas and the Boston Jewish Advocate," *Herzl Year Book 5* (1963), and Louis Lipsky, "Early Days of American Zionism," *PYB* 2 (1946).

In addition to Horace Kallen's own writings—*Culture and Democracy in the United States* (1924) and *Cultural Pluralism and the American Idea* (1956)—see Milton M. Gordon, *Assimilation in American Life* (1964), for an appraisal of cultural pluralism.

On wartime relief for Jews abroad, Oscar Handlin, *A Continuing Task* (1964), discusses the creation of the JDC. The movement for an American Jewish Congress and American Jewish activity at Versailles are analyzed in Oscar I. Janowsky, *The Jews and Minority Rights* (1933).

A comprehensive treatment of Zionism during Wilson's administration is Selig Adler, "The Palestine Question in the Wilson Era," *JSS* 10 (1948). See also Herbert Parzen, "Brandeis and the Balfour Declaration," *Herzl Year Book* 5 (1963); Charles I. Goldblatt, "The Impact of the Balfour Declaration in America," *AJHQ* 57 (1968); *Correspondence on the Advisability of Calling a Conference for the Purpose of Combating Zionism* (1918); Morton Tenzer in *The Immigrants' Influence on Wilson's Peace Policies* (ed. Joseph O'Grady, 1967); Stephen Wise in *The Jewish National Home* (ed. P. Goodman, 1943); and C. Bezalel Sherman, "American Labor Reacts to Zionism," *Herzl Year Book* 5 (1963).

Chapter 3

On the Brandeis-Weizmann split, see George L. Berlin, "The Brandeis-Weizmann Dispute," *AJHQ* 60 (1970). Contemporary materials include *Summary of the Position of the Zionist Organization of America in Conference with Dr. Weizmann and Associates* (1921).

Aspects of American Zionist diplomacy in the 1920s are discussed in Herbert Parzen, "The Lodge-Fish Resolution," *AJHQ* 60 (1970), and Irwin Oder, "American Zionism and the Congressional Resolution of 1922 on Palestine," *PAJHS* 45 (1955). See also U.S. House of Representatives, Committee on Foreign Affairs, *Establishment of a National Home in Palestine: Hearings on H. Con. Res. 52,* 67th Cong. 2d sess., April 1922.

Morton Rosenstock, *Louis Marshall, Defender of Jewish Rights* (1965), discusses the major anti-Semitic eruptions of the decade. Reactions by American Jews appear in Sol Liptzin, *The Jew in American Literature* (1966), and Jacob R. Marcus, "Zionism and the American Jew," *American Scholar* 2 (1933).

Some material on economic and cultural activities can be found in Sherman, *Labor Zionism in America,* and Leo W. Schwarz, "Zionism in America during the Post-War Era" (in *Modern Palestine,* ed. J. Sampter, 1933). On American non-Zionists and the Jewish Agency, see Sam Z. Chinitz, "The Jewish Agency and the Jewish Community in the United States" (M.A. thesis, Columbia University, 1959), and Charles Reznikoff, ed., *Louis Marshall, Champion of Liberty* (1957).

Chapter 4

Jewish "proletarian" novelists are discussed by Liptzin in *The Jew in American Literature* and by Marie Syrkin in "Jewish Awareness in American Literature" (in *The American Jew,* ed. O. Janowsky). Why American Jews were attracted to the left is examined by Nathan Glazer in *The Social Bases of American Communism* (1961).

The study by Samuel Grand, "A History of Zionist Youth Organizations in the United States from Their Inception to 1940" (Unpublished dissertation, Columbia University, 1958), is essential for youth programs and *halutziut.*

Professor Kaplan's philosophy of Reconstructionism was expounded in book form first with *Judaism as a Civilization* (1934). See also Charles S. Liebman, "Reconstructionism in American Jewish Life," *AJYB* 71 (1970).

Material on "latent" Zionism appears in Samuel Dinin, *Zionist Education in the United States* (1944) and Abraham S. Halkin, "Hebrew in Jewish Culture" (in the 1942 ed. of *The American Jew,* ed. O. Janowsky).

For American Jewry's reaction to nazism, demands on the Roosevelt administration, and diplomatic inaction, see Henry L. Feingold, *The Politics of Rescue* (1970); Arthur D. Morse, *While Six Million Died* (1967); and Moshe Gottlieb, "The First of April Boycott and the Reaction of the American Jewish Community," *AJHQ* 57 (1968). The problem of relaxing immigration barriers is treated specifically by David Brody, "American Jewry, the Refugees and Immigration Restriction (1932–1942)," *PAJHS* 45 (1956), and David S. Wyman, *Paper Walls* (1968).

On anti-Semitism in the 1930s, see Donald S. Strong, *Organized Anti-Semitism in America* (1941) and Charles J. Tull, *Father Coughlin and the New Deal* (1965). American views of Jews are analyzed from opinion polls in Charles H. Stember, *Jews in the Mind of America* (1966).

Special studies of Youth Aliyah are Norman Bentwich, *Jewish Youth Comes Home* (1944), and Chasya Pincus, *Come from the Four Winds* (1970). Many memoirs of Youth Aliyah "alumni" were subsequently published. Unity between Zionists and non-Zionists on rebuilding Palestine was the theme of several national conferences beginning in 1935; *Proceedings* of those conferences were published.

Accounts of developments in Palestine are supplemented by the published statements by the ZOA: *Memorandum Submitted to the Palestine Royal Commission on American Interest in the Administration of the Palestine Mandate;* and *A Brief Statement of the Basis and Scope of the*

Right of the United States to Participate in Any Disposition of Palestine; and *The Voice of Christian America: Proceedings of the National Conference on Palestine,* March 9, 1944.

Chapter 5

On relevant aspects of American diplomacy, see *The Memoirs of Cordell Hull* (1948); Selig Adler, *The Isolationist Impulse* (1957); John M. Blum, *From the Morgenthau Diaries: Years of War, 1941–1945* (1967); and James M. Burns, *Roosevelt, The Soldier of Freedom* (1970). Developments in Palestine during the war are treated in Yehuda Bauer, *From Diplomacy to Resistance* (1970).

Studies specifically relating to Roosevelt's policies on Zionism are Samuel Halperin and Irwin Oder, "The United States in Search of a Policy: Franklin D. Roosevelt and Palestine," *Review of Politics* 24 (1962); Selig Adler, "Franklin D. Roosevelt and Zionism—The Wartime Record," *Judaism* 21 (1972); and Richard P. Stevens, *American Zionism and U.S. Foreign Policy, 1942–1947* (1962). Contemporary views are offered by Abba Hillel Silver in "The Political Situation in Zionism," *PYB* 2 (1945–46), and Sumner Welles, *We Need Not Fail* (1948). America's interest in the Middle East in the wake of World War II is traced by J. C. Hurewitz, *Middle East Dilemmas* (1953); Benjamin Schwadran, *The Middle East, Oil and the Great Powers* (1955); E. A. Speiser, *The United States and the Near East* (1951); and Nadav Safran, *The United States and Israel* (1963).

The tactics and ideology of a revitalized American Zionism are detailed in Doreen Bierbrier, "The American Zionist Emergency Council: An Analysis of a Pressure Group," *AJHQ* 60 (1970). See also Herbert Parzen, "American Zionism and the Quest for a Jewish State, 1939–43," *Herzl Year Book* 4 (1962); Solomon Goldman, *Undefeated* (1940); Abba Hillel Silver, *Vision and Victory* (1949); Emanuel Neumann in *PYB* 3 (1947–48) and "The Decline and Rise of Herzlian Zionism," *Herzl Year Book* 3 (1960). Appraisals of Silver are found in Leon I. Feuer, "Abba Hillel Silver: A Personal Memoir," *AJA* 19 (1967), and *The Autobiography of Nahum Goldmann* (1969).

Additional material bearing on congressional action with respect to Zionism is found in Reuben Fink, ed., *America and Palestine* (1945), and U. S. House of Representatives, Committee on Foreign Affairs, *The Jewish National Home in Palestine: Hearings on H. Res. 418 and H. Res. 419,* 78th Cong. 2d sess., 1970 (introd. Ben Halpern).

Chapter 6

Bartley Crum, *Behind the Silken Curtain* (1947), and Richard Crossman, *Palestine Mission* (1947), express the views of two members of the Anglo-American Committee of Inquiry. Lionel Gelber, *America in Britain's Place* (1961), sets the issue against the background of Anglo-American friendship.

On Truman's views and policies, see Jonathan Daniels, *The Man of Independence* (1950), Ian J. Bickerton, "President Truman's Recognition of Israel," *AJHQ* 58 (1968), and Herbert Parzen, "President Truman and the Palestine Quandary: His Initial Experience, April–December 1945," *JSS* 35 (1973). Also of importance are Harry S. Truman, *Memoirs: Years of Trial and Hope* (1956), and the accounts of two members of Truman's administration: *The Forrestal Diaries* (ed. Walter Millis, 1951), and Dean Acheson, *Present at the Creation* (1969). Material relating to the agency's plan for partition is in *The Autobiography of Nahum Goldmann* and Joseph M. Proskauer, *A Segment of My Times* (1950). On partition before the UN, see also David Horowitz, *State in the Making* (1953); Welles, *We Need Not Fail;* Safran, *U.S. and Israel;* Herbert Feis, *The Birth of Israel* (1969); "Two Presidents and a Haberdasher—1948," *AJA* 20 (1968). Popular accounts include Dan Kurzman, *Genesis 1948* (1970); Margaret Truman, *Harry S. Truman* (1973); and Herman Edelsberg, "Harry Truman and Israel," *National Jewish Monthly* 87 (1973). Critical accounts of Zionist political pressures and goals are Alan R. Taylor, *Prelude to Israel* (1959); H. Bradford Westerfield, *Foreign Policy and Party Politics* (1955); Kermit Roosevelt, "The Partition of Palestine," *Middle East Journal* 2 (1948); Virginia C. Gildersleeve, *Many a Good Crusade* (1954); and Robert H. Ferrell, "United States Policy in the Middle East" (in *American Diplomacy in a New Era,* ed. Stephen Kertesz, 1961). Zionism as a factor in the election of 1948 is summarized by Louis L. Gerson in *The Hyphenate in Recent American Politics and Diplomacy* (1964).

Nana Sagi, "The Epic of Aliyah Bet ('Illegal' Immigration) to Palestine 1945–1948," *Midstream* 17 (1971), and David Breslau, ed. *Arise and Build* (1961), discuss the rescue of refugees in defiance of British law. A popular account of American Jewish aid to the Yishuv's preparedness campaign is Leonard Slater, *The Pledge* (1970).

Chapter 7

American relations with Israel, 1948–1967, have not been explored in detail. Schechtman, *The United States and the Jewish State Movement,* carries the story up to 1949. A personal memoir useful for the early years is James G. McDonald, *My Mission in Israel* (1951). Some later material can be found in Safran's two books, *United States and Israel* and *From War to War: The Arab-Israeli Confrontation, 1948–1967* (1969), and in Ernest Stock, *Israel on the Road to Sinai, 1949–1956* (1967). Most accounts examine American interests and diplomacy against the background of the general Middle Eastern area. See J. C. Hurewitz, *Middle East Dilemmas* and *Soviet-American Rivalry in the Middle East* (1969); John S. Badeau, *The American Approach to the Arab World* (1968); John C. Campbell, *Defense of the Middle East* (1960); and American Assembly, *The United States and the Middle East* (1964). Government publications of use are Harry N. Howard, *U.S. Policy in the Near East, South Asia, and Africa* (Dept. of State Publication, 1954); U.S. House of Representatives, Committee on Foreign Affairs, Subcommittee on the Near East, *The Continuing Near East Crisis* (91st Cong. 1st sess., 1969); and Henry A. Byroade, *The Middle East* (Dept. of State Publication, 1954).

Other accounts including material relating specifically to the Suez crisis of 1956 are Herman Finer, *Dulles Over Suez* (1964); E. L. M. Burns, *Between Arab and Israeli* (1963); Earl Berger, *The Covenant and the Sword* (1965); Kennett Love, *Suez: The Twice-Fought War* (1969); Dwight D. Eisenhower, *Waging Peace, 1956–1961* (1965); and M. A. Fitzsimons, "The Suez Crisis and the Containment Policy," *Review of Politics* 19 (1957).

There are even fewer secondary accounts bearing on American Jewish intercession with the government on behalf of Israel. One aspect of this topic is raised in U.S. Senate, Committee on Foreign Relations, *Activities of Nondiplomatic Representatives of Foreign Principals in the United States: Hearings,* 88th Cong. 1st sess., 1963. For some details on the impact of the Suez crisis on the image and behavior of American Jewry, see Lawrence H. Fuchs, *The Political Behavior of American Jews* (1956); Stember, *Jews in the Mind of America;* Moses Rischin, *"Our Own Kind": Voting by Race, Creed, or National Origin;* Judd L. Teller, "The Jewish Vote—Myth or Fact?" *Midstream* 6 (1960); and George Steiner, "How U. S. Jews View the Jewish State," *Life,* August 12, 1957.

Chapter 8

Descriptions of postwar American Jewry are found in C. Bezalel Sherman, "Zionism and the New American Jew," *Forum* 5 (1962); Marshall Sklare, *America's Jews* (1971); Sidney Goldstein, "American

Jewry, 1970: A Demographic Profile," *AJYB* 72 (1971); and Peter I. Rose, ed., *The Ghetto and Beyond* (1969). How the American Jew's position in society shaped his attitudes toward Israel is noted by Sklare and Joseph Greenblum, *The Lakeville Studies,* vol. 1 (1967), and in Sklare, ed., *The Jews* (1958). Sklare also comments on the psychological impact of a Jewish state on American Jews, as do Abraham G. Duker, "The Impact of Zionism on American Jewry" (in *Jewish Life in America,* ed. T. Friedman and R. Gordis, 1955); C. Bezalel Sherman, *Israel and the American Jewish Community* (1951) and *The Jew Within American Society* (1960); Benno Weiser, "Ben Gurion's Dispute with American Zionists," *Commentary* 18 (1954); Abba Hillel Silver, "The Relationship between the American Jewish Community and Israel," *Jewish Social Service Quarterly* 29 (1952); and Arthur Hertzberg, "American Zionism at an Impasse," *Commentary* 8 (1949).

The cleavage between Israelis and American Jews has been the subject of numerous articles. See Maurice Samuel, "The Sundering of Israel and American Jewry," *Commentary* 16 (1953); Judd L. Teller, "American Zionists Move toward Clarity," *Commentary* 12 (1951); Arthur Hertzberg, "The Changing American Rabbinate," *Midstream* 12 (1966); and William R. Polk et al., *Backdrop to Tragedy* (1957).

The historical setting for the cleavage between Israel and American Jews, and the consequent need for reorientation in American Jewish ideology, is explained in Marshall Sklare, *Conservative Judaism* (1955); Simon Halkin, "American Zionism and the State of Israel," *Forum* 1 (1953); Judd L. Teller, "America's Two Zionist Traditions," *Commentary* 20 (1955); and Ben Halpern, "The Idea of a Spiritual Home," *Jewish Frontier* 22 (1955), and *The American Jew* (1956). For relevant developments within American society which influence that reorientation, Will Herberg, *Protestant-Catholic-Jew* (1960), is essential.

Suggestions for a new role for American Zionism are offered in Mordecai M. Kaplan, *A New Zionism* (1959); Daniel Frisch, *Democratization of the American Jewish Community* (1949); and articles in *Congress Weekly,* 1948–49. The theme of Zionist participation in Jewish cultural creativity was sounded immediately after the creation of the state. See, for example, Emanuel Neumann, "Zionism Faces New Tasks," *PYB and Israeli Annual* 4 (1948–49).

American Jewish fund-raising for Israel is discussed in the essay by Joseph Schwartz and Beatrice Vulcan in Janowsky, *The American Jew.* See also Martin Rosenbluth, *Go Forth and Serve* (1961), and David Ben-Gurion, *Rebirth and Destiny of Israel* (1954).

A view of aliyah from the United States is given in Maurice Samuel, "Two Worlds—Two Responses," *Congress Weekly,* May 24, 1954. Ted Berkman's *Cast a Giant Shadow* (1962) is the story of Colonel Marcus; Daniel Spicehandler, an American GI in Palestine on the eve of independence, recounted his experiences in *Let My Right Hand Wither* (1950).

Americans in Israel are discussed by Harold R. Isaacs, *American Jews in Israel* (1967); Ernest Stock, "Americans in Israel," *Midstream* 3 (1957); Hal Lehrman, "When Americans Emigrate to Israel," *Commentary* 13 (1952); M. Z. Frank, "Americans for Israel," *Congress Weekly,* April 24, 1950; and Ira Eisenstein, "Americans in Israel," *Reconstructionist,* Jan. 26, 1951.

Chapter 9

For international developments leading up to the Six-Day War and America's position and interests before and during the war, see Walter Laqueur, *The Road to Jerusalem* (1968); Theodore Draper, *Israel and World Politics* (1968); Love, *Suez: The Twice-Fought War;* Michael Bar-Zohar, *Embassies in Crisis* (1970); Safran, *From War to War;* Campbell. *Defense of the Middle East;* Stock, *Israel on the Road to Sinai;* Badeau, *The American Approach to the Arab World;* William R. Polk, *The United States and the Arab World* (1969); George Lenczowski, ed., *United States Interests in the Middle East* (1968); Hal Kosut, ed., *Israel and the Arabs: The June 1967 War* (1968); U.S. Dept. of State, *United States Policy in the Near East Crisis* (1967); and George Gruen's article in *AJYB* 69 (1968). President Johnson discusses the war in his memoir, *The Vantage Point* (1971); other details are found in Israel Information Services, *The Record of Aggression* (1967).

Public opinion on the Arab-Israeli conflict also appears in the article by Lucy Dawidowicz in *AJYB* 69 (1968), and in Robert Alter, "Israel and the Intellectuals," *A Commentary Report: American Reactions to the Six Day War* (1967). On the New Left, see Martin Peretz, "The American Left and Israel," *A Commentary Report;* Richard L. Rubenstein, *Israel, Zionism and the New Left* (1969); Seymour M. Lipset, *"The Socialism of Fools": The Left, the Jews, and Israel* (1969); and Mordecai S. Chertoff, ed., *The New Left and the Jews* (1971). Judith H. Banki focuses on the churches in *Christian Reactions to the Middle East Crisis* (1968).

Interpretive accounts of American Jewry's response to the war are Arthur Hertzberg, "Israel and American Jewry," and Milton Himmelfarb, "In Light of Israel's Victory," both in *A Commentary Report;* Marshall

Sklare, "Lakeville and Israel: The Six Day War and Its Aftermath," *Midstream* 14 (1968), and Sklare in *The Impact of Israel on American Jewry: Twenty Years Later* (1969).

Chapter 10

The meaning of Israel for American Jews is thoughtfully discussed in Jacob Neusner, *American Judaism: Adventure in Modernity* (1972); Charles S. Liebman, *The Ambivalent American Jew* (1973); and Marshall Sklare, *America's Jews* (1971). See also Marie Syrkin, "How Israel Affects American Jews," *Midstream* 19 (1973).

Index